Christmas, 1980

For my dear friend Susan

May your explorations
lead you to new
heights
      love,
      Merna

Adventures in
Archaeology

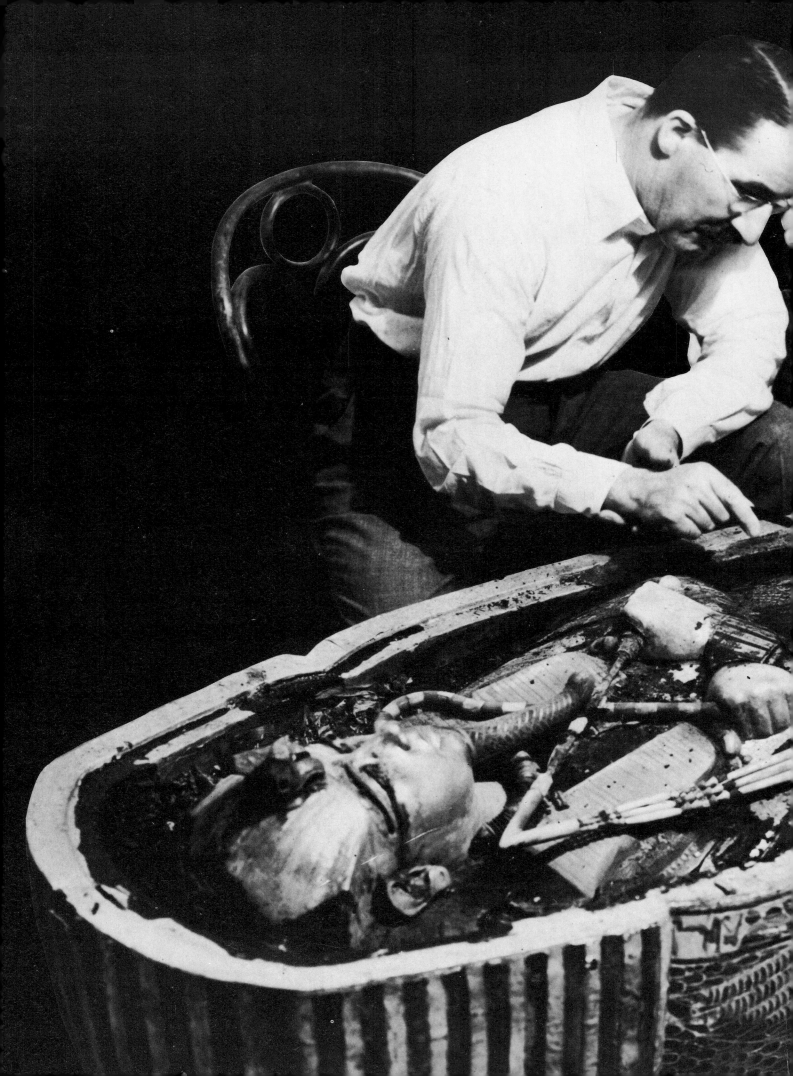

Adventures in
Archaeology
Anne Ward

Larousse and Co., Inc.
New York

First published in the United States by
Larousse and Co., Inc.,
572 Fifth Avenue
New York, N.Y. 10036
© 1977 The Hamlyn Publishing Group Limited,
London · New York · Sydney · Toronto

Library of Congress Catalog Card No. 77–70576
ISBN 0–88332–077–0

Filmset by Tradespools Ltd.,
Frome, Somerset, England
Printed in Great Britain by Cox & Wyman Ltd.,
London, Fakenham and Reading

Contents

Introduction: the science of archaeology   7

Theseus and the Minotaur: new light on the legend   19

Pompeii and Herculaneum   31

The Rosetta Stone deciphered   47

The jungle cities of the Maya   57

Chichén Itzá: treasures from the sacred well   77

The epic of Gilgamesh   85

The mysterious civilisation of the Indus Valley   97

Jericho: the first city dwellers   109

Tutankhamun: the boy king   123

The Dead Sea Scrolls   139

Fakes, frauds and forgeries   149

Bibliography   158

Acknowledgments   159

Index   160

Introduction:
the science of archaeology

A Victorian humorist once remarked that 'give me back the good old days of fifty years ago' has been the cry ever since Adam's 51st birthday; and it is certainly true that nostalgia for the past forms a conspicuous part of a great many people's natural make-up. This characteristic seems to be particularly strong during periods of rapid change and advance, which suggests that it may arise in part from a need for the security of that which has already been tried, proved and survived, as opposed to the perilous excitements of a dauntingly unpredictable future. There is more to it, however, than simple escapism; the human race, like every individual member of it, is an amalgam of its total experience, and we cannot know what we are, or what we may become, unless we know what we have been. Archaeology is therefore a reflection of man's need to understand himself.

A great deal of heat has been generated from time to time in discussions about the precise nature and meaning of archaeology. For practical purposes a simple definition will suffice: it is a study of the past based on surviving material remains.

Rational enquiry into the origins of man as opposed to romantic nostalgia or mythological thinking was initiated by the Greeks, who were the founders of so many intellectual disciplines. Their speculations were perceptive and thoughtful but confined, for the most part, to theory without practical application. There are records, however, of enterprises which fall well within the modern definition of archaeology. The historian Thucydides tells how the Athenians formed deductions about the inhabitants of Delos from the burial methods and grave goods they found in tombs on the island, and since contemporary archaeologists still regard tombs as perhaps the most useful source of evidence, they would fully endorse the Greeks' methods and conclusions. Where they would differ is in their subsequent handling of the finds. The Athenians seem to have had no notion of preserving the ancient remains, while today's scholars would employ every resource of science, skill and technology to save all the fragments.

The Greeks, then, studied the past but made no attempt to amass tangible evidence. The Romans, on the other hand, collected Greek antiquities avidly from an early date. Most men of wealth and power had their own private art galleries, and they set about the plundering of Greece with the methodical thoroughness which they brought to bear on all their activities. Ship after ship left Piraeus loaded not only with statues and other works of art but even with sections of dismantled buildings down to column drums and carved capitals. The Romans were rapacious, and their interest in ancient art was purely that of the dilettante collector who is chiefly interested in the prestige and price of his pieces. However, their covetousness served one useful purpose. Many masterpieces which were destroyed in antiquity are still known to us through Roman copies, and in at least one case the original has been recovered because of the Romans' acquisitive zeal. When the wreck of a Roman treasure ship was investigated on the sea bed off Mahdia in Tunisia it was found to be full of statues, including some by known masters, and of architectural elements on their way from Greece to adorn the villa of some influential soldier or senator.

When the Roman empire finally disintegrated and the Dark Ages spread over Europe, antiquarian pursuits were totally abandoned. There was little change during the Middle Ages, for although neither scholarship nor culture were lacking there was still little curiosity about earlier times, possibly because this was one of the long static eras of minimal change and progress when no one felt a need for the security of the past. At first sight the medieval period, with its ceaseless power struggles and plagues, seems anything but stable. This turmoil, however, existed only on a superficial level. Although the peasant might not be sure from one day to the next who ruled the principality he lived in, this cannot have affected him very much. He worked his field, paid his taxes and never looked much farther than the manor to which he belonged and which regulated his earthly life, and the Church which dictated his

opposite By the mid-18th century, knowledge of classical civilisations was already considerable, and wealthy patrons of the arts were avid in their pursuit of antique marbles and statuary. The painting by Johann Zoffany, 'Charles Towneley and his Friends', shows one of Britain's foremost collectors (on the right) with his antiquarian colleagues. Towneley Hall Art Gallery and Museum, Burnley.

every spiritual attitude. His place in the total scheme of things and that scheme itself in this world and the next was fixed, immutable and unquestionable, as it was for the lord of the manor, the priest and the scholar. The finest minds might wrestle in interminable theological debate on such knotty questions as how many angels could stand on the point of a pin, but they expended no speculation on the historical records or material remains of their ancestors. Nearly all thought was confined within the bounds of a religious canon which embraced every aspect of life and death, which decreed that all things were as they were because the divine will had ordered it so, and to question this will or seek to change its effects was blasphemy or heresy.

This habit of unquestioning acceptance had become so strong that a major intellectual, social and artistic upheaval was needed to sweep it away, and just such a force appeared and rose to a brilliant zenith in 15th-century Italy. The Renaissance was much more than the text-book picture of an upsurge of classicism triggered off by the rediscovery of ancient manuscripts brought to the west by refugees from the siege of Constantinople—it was an entirely new way of looking at life, examining it for the first time in centuries by humanist rather than mystical criteria. Until the Reformation and Counter-Reformation placed a fresh curb on this freedom of thought, man might look with his own eyes, think with his own mind and act according to his own conscience, an attitude which brought with it radical changes in every field of endeavour to which it was applied.

One of the most immediate results was a re-awakening of interest in classical cultures. In the forefront of this movement were the great scholars, artists and prince-patrons, whose influence did so much to encourage and disseminate the new learning that enthusiasm rose until it was said that Greek could be heard in the streets of Florence as often as Tuscan (one feels that there must be more than a touch of wish-fulfilment in this statement), and that Plato was regarded as a sort of demi-god. It is a pity that all this antiquarian zeal contained so little of the spirit of conservation; but to the Renaissance princes, like the Romans before them, being cultivated meant being a collector, and collecting meant the ruthless pillage of ancient monuments and sites. More ancient buildings were probably wrecked by the antiquity-loving classicists of the Renaissance than by all the Goths, Huns and Vandals of history put together.

Despite the architectural mayhem wrought by these dedicated collectors, they had their value in amassing, describing and cataloguing vast numbers of ancient *objets d'art* which were thus preserved for the attention of later more scholarly antiquarians; not that these pieces always survived in the condition in which they were found, for the next two centuries were the heyday of the 'improver'. With an arrogance which strikes the modern observer as little short of devastating, sculptors would decide that if the ancient artist had not practised certain principles of design and craftsmanship then he should have done, and it was up to their own

The Florentines of the Renaissance were fascinated by Etruscan art, believing that ancient Tuscany had a quite different civilisation from that of Rome. This bronze, known as the Arezzo Chimera, was found in 1554, acquired by Cosimo I, grand duke of Tuscany, and restored by Benvenuto Cellini. Museo Archeologico, Florence.

8

more enlightened age to correct these short-comings. It is hard to reconcile this attitude with their much-vaunted reverence for the departed glories of the golden classical age, but many artists quite distinguished enough to know better seem to have had no hesitation in hacking away at an ancient masterpiece until its own creator would scarcely have recognised it, and showing the keenest self-satisfaction at their depredations. Although there was now a lively interest in the ancient world, it only covered great works of art and did not extend to the everyday life of former civilisations, nor did it include any but the dimmest notions of reconstructing the past from its artifacts.

The Age of Reason brought with it some slight stirrings in this direction, but with it came another influence which led simultan-

of sequences of events as reflected by the artifacts, and Winckelmann's work was a significant move towards this goal. Others were quick to follow this lead, and a coherent picture of man's past gradually began to form. There were a lot of hazy passages in this picture, and still more blanks, but only one more essential element remained to be added before archaeology could be pursued as an organised study. This was supplied in the early 19th century.

What the discipline needed was a recognisable chronological framework depending on material evidence rather than historical dates, which could be applied to all cultures including those with no written history. The Danish scholar Thomsen and his successor Worsaae produced this when they worked out the three Ages—Stone, Bronze and Iron. These ages indicated stages of technological development and were flexible enough to cover any culture at almost any date. Being independent of historical time

opposite The 1st-century BC Greek marble, Laocoön, was rediscovered during the Renaissance in an imperial Roman palace on the Esquiline, and had a profound impact on contemporary artists. Vatican Museums.

left This bronze statue, probably by Praxiteles, is one of the many Greek works recovered from wrecked ships; it was found in the Bay of Marathon in 1925 and is now in the National Museum, Athens.

eously to a widening of the scope of archaeology and to frequent grotesque misapplications of its function. This was the rise of Romanticism. Devotees of this cult of heightened sensibility and unchecked emotional indulgence found the classical world, with its tranquil and rational orderliness, too coldly intellectual a study, and they turned eagerly to the more northerly 'barbarian' cultures, which seemed to embody all their favourite elements. Blasted heaths, crumbling shrines, horror, mystery and a hint of blood sacrifice were almost *de rigueur*, and these could be more readily attributed to cultures of which very little was known, which left few, if any, written records, and in which savagery and barbarism seemed the dominant characteristics. Celtic graves, barrows, Viking burials and above all the great megalithic monuments such as Stonehenge and Avebury were enthusiastically explored. Gentlemen who were fortunate enough to have such remains on their estates conducted investigations and offered interpretations which often had a good deal to do with the current rather gory sense of melodrama and very little to do with the facts; but however misguided these activities and some of their results might be, at least they paved the way for future studies by raising a keen general interest in non-classical antiquities.

At this time a considerable assortment of facts about the ancient world had been amassed, but they formed unrelated pockets of knowledge with no interaction or mutual relevance. The German scholar, Johann Winckelmann, inspired by his observations on the sites of Pompeii and Herculaneum, was one of the first to assemble the available information into a corpus and to arrange it in chronological order. Archaeology is very largely concerned with the establishing

A sunken Roman ship found by Greek sponge-divers at Mahdia in Tunisia in 1907 proved to be full of Greek works of art on their way to adorn the villas of leading Roman citizens. This bronze statue of a winged Eros-like youth was among them. The contents of the treasure-ship now fill five rooms in the Bardo Museum in Tunis—a testament to the Romans' collecting zeal.

During the 17th century, the French traveller, Jean Chardin, explored ancient Persia, and a remarkably accurate view of the ruins of Persepolis appeared in his *Voyages en Perse*, published in 1711.

Divers working near Naples to salvage Roman amphorae from the seabed.

they could coexist simultaneously in different civilisations, as the Stone Age Aborigines in 19th-century Australia did with their Iron Age European immigrant contemporaries. When the evidence called for greater precision these eras could be broken down into appropriate subdivisions such as the Old, Middle and New Stone Ages (or Paleolithic, Mesolithic and Neolithic periods) or the Early, Middle and Late Bronze Ages. The Iron Age is not usually subdivided in this way, perhaps because most cultures do not reach this level of technical advancement until they are fully literate, or at least in association with cultures which are, and which therefore have written histories to pinpoint dates. There is also a possibility that the Iron Age cannot be finally systematised for the simple reason that we are still in it – unless future archaeologists prefer to classify the present decade as Early Atomic I.

The basic idea of dating the artifacts of any culture in relationship to each other rather than in terms of absolute historical time once established, provided a framework which could be adapted to any place or era. Different civilisations could be connected to each other by stylistic links or occasional imported objects, and the whole complex could sometimes be pegged down by a rare absolute date derived from a better-documented culture. In this way the outlines of archaeology were laid down, expanded and filled in by generations of scholars.

Progress, especially when it is rapid, is seldom smoothly achieved in any major discipline, and 19th-century archaeology was no exception. There was no obstacle to advancement in the study of the classical civilisations and those of Western Asia, where great discoveries and brilliant decipherments followed each other in breathtaking profusion. The chief hurdle lay in the path of Stone Age studies, and it was provided by no less an authority than the first book

The battle was fought over several decades as the evidence accumulated and the upholders of tradition found themselves forced to increasingly far-fetched explanations of these intractable facts, but the point of no return came in 1859 with the publication of Darwin's *Origin of the Species*. This monumental work of authoritative scholarship struck at the long-cherished idea that man was not just another type of animal but a sort of angel, made in God's image and subject to none of the factors affecting mere brutes. Darwin and his archaeological and anthropological followers did not achieve immediate acceptance – indeed, as late as the 1920s an American schoolteacher was prosecuted for teaching evolution instead of the Genesis story of creation – but their ideas were in the ascendant and it could only be a matter of time before they were endorsed by the vast majority.

of the Old Testament. Church dignitaries had worked out that the creation of the world took place in 4004 BC, on 23 October to be exact (it seems a pity that the ingenious gentleman who produced this information was not able to establish the precise time of day). This raised disturbing questions in the minds of sincere believers who, exploring caves and gravel pits, came across human remains and implements in association with the bones of extinct animals known to have existed long before the date assigned to the Flood.

As soon as this scientific view of man's past was more or less established, traces of it were sought and found outside the framework of the Biblical and classical studies which had defined it for so long. In the Americas, the Far East, India, Australasia and the Pacific islands more evidence began to emerge, pushing back the frontiers of knowledge and illuminating with fresh information the civilisations which were already known and explored. For several decades this pattern continued largely unaltered, with explorers and excavators in the

An impression of an 18th-century excavation in Greece, from Leroy's *Ruines des plus beaux monuments de la Grèce*, published in 1758.

opposite top A fascination
with the manifestations of
'barbarian' cultures, such
as Celtic graves and
megalithic monuments,
characterised the Roman-
tic movement.

The Forum, centre of
civic and religious life in
ancient Rome, fell into
decay after the decline of
the Empire, and was
neglected even during the
Renaissance. In the 18th
century, however, system-
atic excavations began,
greatly increasing our
knowledge of the past.

field producing an ever-increasing body of facts, and scholars in museums and libraries consolidating the discipline by their work of evaluation, interpretation and classification, the two aspects being frequently carried out by the same man. The next really significant advance did not take place until after the Second World War, when archaeology developed a strongly scientific aspect with the application of physics and chemistry to the problems of dating.

The big break-through came with the discovery of radio-carbon (or carbon-14) dating. This process was evolved, and published in 1949 by an American atomic chemist named W. F. Libby. He reasoned that all living things, plant or animal, are equally subject to a per-petual bombardment of cosmic rays, from which they absorb carbon-14 in quantities which are kept stable throughout their lives, so that as long as they live they are all equally radio-active. When death supervenes, however, absorption stops and the radio-active substances begin to break down. The time this disintegration takes to reduce the carbon-14 in organic material by half is known as the half-life of the isotope; in the case of carbon-14 it lasts for 5568 years. Thus by measuring the amount of carbon-14 remaining in any organic substance the date at which it ceased to live could be established. Libby and his colleagues experimented for years to perfect their method, and then applied it to several different ancient samples of known

date. It proved accurate within 10 per cent.

Radio-carbon analysis is not a miracle worker. A great many adjustments have to be made to allow for varying conditions which may affect the process, and there is always a margin of error which grows progressively larger with older specimens. In the case of well-documented civilisations such as those of classical Greece and Rome this margin is large enough to make the application of the method impractical. There is no point in establishing a date which may be, for example, 100 years out each way for a culture with pottery sequences which can be dated within a five-year span. For older pre-literate eras or suspected fakes, however, it can be invaluable. It has not changed the face of archaeology so drastically as many people once thought it would, but it has provided some enormously useful starting points, checks and corrections.

Libby's example was soon followed by other scientists. A few years later it was demonstrated that what carbon-14 could do for organic materials, potassium-argon could do for minerals. Potassium is a substance which occurs in nearly every mineral on earth in fairly measurable quantities. Its isotope, potassium-40, has a half-life of a thousand million years during the course of which a known percentage turns into argon-14. By measuring the relative proportions of potassium-40 and argon-40 in any mineral its age can be established. As this process begins, on the whole, where radio-carbon leaves off, it is particularly useful in dating the environment of very early man. For instance, an application of potassium-argon dating revealed that the remains of our first ancestors in the Olduvai Gorge in Africa were about 750,000 years old.

Of the two recently evolved methods for dating baked clay, one depends on knowing exactly where it was fired. All clay contains some proportion of iron particles, and each of these is magnetic, like a tiny compass needle. In the natural clay they are scattered about at random, but when the clay is heated to a high temperature they are set free to move, and accordingly they align themselves with the earth's magnetic field, where they are fixed as the clay cools again. The magnetic north varies slightly with the passage of time, and when one is certain exactly whereabouts the clay was at the time of firing it is possible to work out from the alignment of particles where the magnetic north lay at this time. The shift of the magnetic north is well charted, so this can fix the date of firing for such immovable objects as kilns or burnt buildings.

Potsherds, which can be justifiably called the archaeologist's best friend, are far too portable for archaeomagnetism to be safely applied to their dating, but they can be dated with increasing accuracy by a recent process known as

thermoluminescence. Long ago it was observed that if a piece of terracotta is heated red-hot it seems to glow with extra brightness, as if it had some source of energy in addition to the heat of the fire, and recent research has discovered the reason for this. As living substances absorb carbon from cosmic rays, so do minerals absorb extra electrons. When clay is fired these extra electrons are given off, creating the extra energy which causes the material to glow so brightly, and incidentally setting the level of extra electrons in the clay back to zero again. The process of absorption then recommences, and continues until the pot re-encounters a high degree of heat. If the sherd is taken to the laboratory it can be heated to the required

It was not until the 19th century that archaeology became an organised study; before this time it had lacked a chronological framework which could be applied to all cultures. Detailed study of flint workings enabled scholars to construct such a framework from material evidence long before modern dating methods were available.
Musée des Antiquités Nationales, St Germain en Laye.

Electrical resistance surveying makes use of variations in the humidity of the soil: the wetter the soil the more readily the current will pass through it. Thus above ditches or pits the electrical resistance will drop, while above a buried wall it will rise. The illustration shows the instrument on its tripod and the five electrodes which are stuck into the ground at intervals of one tenth of a metre. These are connected to the transformer by separate wires.

temperature and the thermoluminescence (extra heat and light) it gives off in the process can be measured. Once this is known it is not difficult to establish how long it would take for pottery to absorb this quantity of extra electrons and thus to discover how long ago the last firing took place.

All these processes are subject to a number of influences which may affect the accuracy of the dating and which therefore have to be taken into account and allowed for when the measurements are made, since they introduce significant variations. Another much older dating system which has recently been given a new lease of life does not include these modifying elements, but it is nothing like so universally applicable. This is dendrochronology, or dating by tree-rings. Every tree trunk consists, in section, of a number of concentric rings, one of which is added with every year of the tree's life. In good years when there is plenty of water and growth

One of the most important tasks of archaeology is the precise dating of objects, which has been greatly facilitated by advances in science. This equipment, in the research laboratory at the British Museum, is required for the synthesis of benzene which is used in the process of radio-carbon dating.

conditions are favourable the ring is wide but in poor years it will be narrow, and every tree subject to the same climate will show exactly the same pattern of rings. At the turn of this century an American scholar named Douglass had already realised the possible significance of the number and pattern of tree-rings, and was beginning to amass a collection of records against which trees of unknown date could be checked. After 30 years of work he had established a basic tree-ring pattern for the south-west United States which stretched back to AD 700 and which, among other advantages, provided an invaluable cross-check for later experiments in radio-carbon dating.

For some years after Douglass's death dendrochronology was at a standstill. It was dramatically revived with the discovery of that venerable patriarch of trees, the bristle-cone pine, which grows in such areas as the Snake Range of Nevada and the White Mountains of eastern California. Its life-span makes the ancient oaks of England and even the great California red-woods look like mere saplings, for one aged specimen, the oldest living thing on earth, is now known to be an incredible 4900 years old, and still growing. Cores, drilled with the utmost care to avoid damage to the health and growth of the tree, provide a basic dendrochronology for the whole area from a single tree, without any necessity for cross references which always introduce the possibility of error. Unfortunately this dating system is a strictly local phenomenon, applicable only to wood from the immediate neighbourhood where one set of climatic conditions prevail. In the United Kingdom, for instance, it is virtually useless. The climate is so erratic that trees growing only a few miles apart can exhibit entirely different growth characteristics.

Nowadays there is a slight tendency to regard these marvels of modern science and others like them as the infallible answer to all archaeological problems. In some respects, of course, this is true. A forged modern pot, for example, can fool an expert but it cannot deceive a thermoluminescence counter. However, machines and processes are only as good as the people who operate them, and it should never be forgotten that the establishment of a fact is an isolated phenomenon. Only when the significance of this fact and its relationship to others is evaluated and understood does it become truly important in the never-ending work of deducing man's past. Archaeology has been and always will be many things to many people – some of their stories are told in the following pages – but among these multifarious facets one must always be constant: if it is not about people, for people and by people, it is little more than a handful of dust.

In modern times, many different methods are used in surveying for archaeological sites. Vertical aerial surveying eliminates much tedious fieldwork, and by providing a plan view of the ground, often shows up features which could not be distinguished at ground level.

Restoration is also a vital part of archaeology. Ancient buildings often need repair, and to preserve their authenticity, archaeologists take care to reproduce the original materials. At Mohenjodaro in the Indus Valley, experts are reshaping bricks to replace diseased masonry.

Theseus and the Minotaur: new light on the legend

In its classical form the legend of Theseus and the Minotaur includes a few elements which are not entirely suitable for the nursery school, but in a slightly edited version the story is almost as much part of Western folklore as that of Cinderella or the Sleeping Beauty – and just about as widely believed.

Once upon a time – it begins as all good legends should – the great king Minos ruled the island of Crete. Wishing to please the sea-god Poseidon, the king planned to offer a sacrifice for which Poseidon provided a magnificent white bull. Minos coveted the splendid creature and decided to conceal it among his own herd and substitute another for sacrifice; but the gods are not easily deceived and his presumption in withholding divine property was punished in a hideously appropriate fashion. His wife Queen Pasiphaë, driven mad by the angry Poseidon, developed an unnatural passion for the white bull, mated secretly with it, and conceived the Minotaur, a monster with a bull's head and a human body which fed on human flesh. To hide this dreadful hybrid Minos employed the inventor Daedalus, who designed and built the Labyrinth, an underground maze of such complexity that no one who entered it ever found the way out again. In the middle was the Minotaur's lair, and here it devoured the victims whom Minos demanded as tribute from the lesser nations around Crete.

Among these unfortunate people were the Athenians, who had to supply seven youths and seven maidens every ninth year. Theseus, son of the king of Athens, was still a young man, but he had already proved himself in a number of heroic exploits, and when the tribute year came around again he decided that he must go to Crete with the chosen victims and confront the monster. When the young people from Athens arrived, Minos' daughter Ariadne fell in love with Theseus and determined to help him. Coming to him by night, she provided him with a sword to fight the Minotaur and a large ball of thread. He fastened one end of the thread to the doorpost at the entrance of the Labyrinth and, unrolling it as he went along, laid a trail by which he could find his way out again. Ariadne's devices were successful. Theseus made his way into the monster's lair, fought and killed it and hurried back along the lifeline of thread to where Ariadne was awaiting him. They fled together and made their escape by ship before morning. Their story being a legend, not a fairy-tale, they did not live happily ever after; but their subsequent vicissitudes, though colourful enough, are something of an anticlimax compared with the great fight with the Minotaur in the heart of the Labyrinth.

It makes a good story, but no one would have taken it for history: no one, that is, until a team of archaeologists began to excavate in Crete about the beginning of this century and learned, not for the first time, that it is never safe to rule out the possibility of truth in even the most bizarre legend. Heinrich Schliemann, the grocer's boy turned millionaire whose commercial success alone might have seemed achievement enough for one man's lifetime, had already given the academic world two startling lessons in the advantages to be gained from taking the ancients at their word. He began, in 1870, by revealing the site of Homer's Troy at Hissarlik on the Dardanelles, basing his deductions almost entirely on the topographical details in the *Iliad*; but even this triumph was not sufficient for the indefatigable Schliemann. In 1876 he turned his attention to the Bronze Age ruins of Mycenae at the head of the plain of Argos in Greece.

There was no problem here in locating the site; it was a well-known tourist attraction, and had been one to the classical Greeks, including a 2nd-century traveller named Pausanias. His description of Greece has proved to be an invaluable source of information to scholars from his own day to this, but Schliemann was the first to notice – and believe – his mention of a group of richly endowed royal tombs within the fortification walls. Once again he went to the spot indicated by the ancient authority, and was vindicated by the discovery of a group of shaft graves containing skeletons and a breathtaking treasure of golden jewels, weapons, vessels,

opposite Sir Arthur Evans, discoverer, excavator, codifier and publisher of the Minoan civilisation, devoted most of his life and the resources of his great personal fortune to the immense task of making Crete part of the world's archaeological heritage. He is shown here surrounded by a few of the innumerable treasures he had unearthed from the mound of Knossos, holding the bull's head rhyton.

Heinrich Schliemann's claim to have discovered a new world for archaeology was no idle boast, for until his day scholars had believed that the heroic age depicted in the poems of Homer was a figment of the poetic imagination, and nothing was known of the complex cultures of the Bronze Age Aegean.

The search for the Minoans began with the investigation of the Grave Circle at Mycenae, where Schliemann discovered a group of royal burials accompanied by fabulous treasures of gold, some of which could not be attributed stylistically to the local culture.

ornaments and disturbingly individualised portrait masks. 'I have gazed on the face of Agamemnon', he announced jubilantly. He was wrong by several centuries—but this does not detract from the importance of his discovery, which confirmed the existence of a civilisation predating that of classical Greece by 1000 years.

Schliemann's revelations were soon followed by others, which showed that the Mycenaean culture had extended throughout the whole of Greece. As scholars studied the finds, however, they became increasingly aware of an oddly disparate influence which was particularly strong among the earlier material, including the shaft-grave treasure. Local workmanship of this date undeniably had a striking barbaric splendour, but on close examination the technique proved to be clumsy and the design awkward and stiff, curiously lacking in grace and vitality. Among these ponderous pieces the mysterious alien element stood out unmistakably, with its unerring sense of composition, confident mastery

of difficult metallurgical processes, and wonderfully joyous and vivid naturalism. Scholars speculated and puzzled over its source for years, but it was not until the last decade of the century that Schliemann's unfailing nose for a good find began to point in the direction of Crete. He was actually in the process of negotiating the purchase of the mound at Knossos when he died in 1890.

Meanwhile another archaeologist was reaching similar conclusions, but the route by which Arthur Evans travelled to Knossos was the antithesis of Schliemann's. Son of a rich father, he received a conventional education at Harrow and Brasenose College, Oxford, after which he spent some time at Göttingen University. At first his interest centred on the Balkans, but he was later drawn to Crete by a factor which, in anyone less gifted, might have been a serious disability. Arthur Evans was severely myopic, but although his long-distance vision was impaired his short sight enabled him to focus with

minute clarity on detailed miniature work, and this microscopic scrutiny he brought to bear on the tiny carved stones worn by many Cretan peasant women as milk charms. A close study of these amulets led him to the conclusion that they belonged to an ancient culture which was the only possible source of the unidentified influence in Mycenaean art. From this time onwards the resources of his great wealth and formidable scholarship were entirely devoted to the Cretan civilisation. He bought the enormous site of Knossos in 1899 and began his life's work of excavating it.

Few archaeologists have laboured with such skill and diligence, and few have been better rewarded; for his work revealed that Knossos was the palatial centre of a Bronze Age culture which, predating that of the Mycenaeans by several centuries, was one of the earliest and certainly one of the most brilliant in Europe. Fresh discoveries soon followed. A French team found another palace at Mallia and the Italians

The site of the palace of Phaistos is the only one which might have been chosen with an eye to defence – but it is more likely that the spectacular mountain scenery surrounding it was the operative consideration. Entry to the palace was provided by a flight of low, wide steps leading through a hall set at right angles to the north of the central court, from which the massif of Mount Ida can be seen in the distance.

On the east side of the central courtyard at Knossos was a complex of apartments apparently set aside to be the private quarters of the royal family. The ground slopes fairly steeply at this point, and the rooms are located on several different levels, joined by a magnificent staircase built round a square light well. The characteristic Cretan column, thick, stubby and tapering inwards at the bottom, supports the open side of the multi-storey stair.

one at Phaistos, where they are still conducting and publishing excavations which yearly enlarge the sum of knowledge in the field of Cretan archaeology. Fine villas have been found at Haghia Triada, Tylissos and Nerou Chani, the little town of Gournia has been explored and harbour installations at Amnisos were traced in the 1930s. In more recent years a royal tomb with a rich collection of Late Minoan jewllery was found at Archanes, a miniature palace at Zakro, and a Minoan 'Pompeii' in the form of a provincial settlement on the island of Santorini which was overwhelmed in an appalling eruption during the first quarter of the 15th century BC.

Year after year Evans excavated, recorded and studied the findings from Knossos, collating and comparing them with subsequent discoveries on other sites and finally publishing his conclusions in an encyclopaedic work entitled *The Palace of Minos at Knossos*. Some of his ideas have necessarily been modified in the light of later research (for instance, the Linear B tablets from the latest levels of the palace were not deciphered in his lifetime) but his book is still the 'bible' of Minoan studies.

The culture he described was extraordinarily harmonious and attractive. Perhaps its closest analogy is that of medieval Venice, for the Minoans, too, transpired to be art-loving, peaceful merchant princes in a world largely given over to battle and conquest. Like the gracious palazzi of Venice, the Cretan palaces lay hospitably open without a trace of rampart or fortification, and like the Venetians, the Minoans lived in a setting of unparalleled beauty and luxury; it is likely, however, that the earlier people, with their numerous bathrooms, piped water supplies and efficient sanitary engineering, enjoyed a far higher degree of personal cleanliness than the Venetians.

The excavations showed that the palace started as a number of separate buildings grouped around an open courtyard. The latter was practically the only feature which remained constant throughout the Bronze Age, for as time passed the palace was extended and beautified, the scattered buildings were linked together under one roof and further storeys added to the original structure in an apparently haphazard conglomeration. The Minoans were clearly undismayed by the frequent earthquakes which shook the island and sometimes flattened

parts of the palace; they merely made another sacrifice to the huge square support-pillar which stood (and still stands) in a basement shrine, and enthusiastically seized the opportunity for even more extensive rebuilding.

During the last phase of Minoan occupation the palace was nothing less than a rambling

town under a single roof. The oblong courtyard remained unchanged, but the apartments round it had now arrived at their final peak of perfection. South of the court lay the ceremonial entrance, a long corridor of ramps and stairs, the walls splendid with frescoes of processions in honour of the great goddess. The Minoan painter's palette was limited, but his vision was not, and the passage must have made a striking impact on the guest walking up it for the first time while these brilliant figures, so stately yet so vitally human, silently kept pace with him. The living quarters of the royal family lay on the east of the courtyard. This complex, several storeys high, was united by a fine staircase winding round a light-well, and included sitting rooms, bedrooms, bathrooms and even that greatest Minoan rarity, a guardroom. The walls were bright with frescoes, more playful and less hieratic than those of the ceremonial apartments, and though furnishings were sparse, there were tubs of flowers to scent the air, handsome oil lamps of stone and bronze, and portable charcoal braziers for cool weather. Some idea of how the inhabitants looked was provided by the 'fashion-plates' of ancient Crete—little faience

By the 4th century BC Knossos was no more than a minor provincial town, but it had its own mint, and the coins issued there reflect the persistence of folk-memory. A stater dating to 350–325 shows a stylised labyrinth, already transmuted into its familiar modern form of a maze, since the actuality of the ancient palace had, by this time, been lost and forgotten for centuries. British Museum, London.

In its great days the palace at Knossos housed a vast population of wealthy aristocrats whose daily needs required huge quantities of stores. These were kept in a honeycomb of underground cellars beneath the west wing, where rows of enormous jars, each taller than the average Minoan, held the oil, wine and corn on which the island's life and commercial prosperity depended.

At Knossos even the great goddess and her high priestesses dressed in the height of current fashion. Apart from her ritual headgear, this faience figurine is wearing the clothes of a typical lady of the court, with a short-sleeved, low-cut jacket, the tightly laced waist which was so much admired in both sexes by the Cretans, and a long skirt made of a number of embroidered, jewelled and colourful flounces beneath a decorative apron. Archaeological Museum, Heraklion.

Representations of Minoan religion are numerous, but in the absence of written explanations, its exact nature remains a mystery. One of the most explicit scenes occurs on a late painted plaster sarcophagus from Haghia Triada which shows a priestess pouring a libation at an altar flanked by tall double axes. Behind her stands another woman, crowned and carrying a pair of vessels, and only then, occupying what appears to be a subordinate position, male musicians and other celebrants and offerings.

figurines of stylish goddesses or priestesses in gowns which, for sophisticated daring and elaboration, could vie with anything from *ancien régime* Versailles. The ladies of the palace wore close-fitting bodices cut low enough to expose the breasts and tight-laced to a handspan waist; skirts made in several flounces, stiff with embroidery and spangled with gold. Their hair was dressed in short curls over the forehead and crown and long ringlets down the back, heavily ornamented with beads, ribbons, diadems and pins of gold, while their pert little heart-shaped faces were by no means innocent of cosmetics.

The Minoans, who were obviously far more practical about such matters than the designers of Versailles, located the kitchens close to the living rooms of the royal family, and beyond them were the quarters of the servants and the army of craftsmen who must have laboured night and day supplying the demand for beautiful objects.

West of the courtyard were the ceremonial reception halls, the shrines, lustral basins and the ritual chambers, and the dimly lit throne room where the simple stone chair of Minos stands to this day under its guard of painted griffins. Finally, there is the north entrance to the court, a narrow passage overlooked by a pillared portico where Evans found the remains of a fresco which was to throw a dazzling new light on the legend of Theseus and the Minotaur.

No subsequent discoveries have eclipsed or even begun to rival the importance of Evans's

Very few, if any, buildings of an exclusively religious function have been identified in Crete, and it may perhaps be assumed that the palace itself was the centre of the cult, with the monarch also holding a priestly function. Private homes, however, often had small domestic shrines, and these crude mass-produced figurines of votaries or goddesses frequently occur, especially during the last Minoan age. Archaeological Museum, Heraklion.

In the last age of the Minoan civilisation, when the island appears to have been under the domination of an alien ruler from mainland Greece, the palace at Knossos was briefly reoccupied, and a restricted rebuilding programme was implemented. The throne room with its ancient chair of state was frescoed very much in the mainland manner with recumbent griffins and stiffly regimented stylised lilies. The originals are now in the museum at Heraklion, and modern replicas have been put in their places.

excavation progressed, the more bulls he found, many of them engaged in an activity which seemed inexplicable till the discovery of the 'Toreador Fresco' in an east court provided an answer even more fantastic than the question. The fresco was badly damaged and much of it was missing. The restorer's work, too, leaves something to be desired, but the gist of the subject is clear. It shows a huge brown and white bull with two girls and a boy, all dressed alike in the fashionable Minoan male clothing of a tightly belted codpiece, pointed footwear laced up to the calves and a lavish array of jewellery on their necks and arms and in their long black hair. One of the girls is standing on tiptoe, arms outstretched, behind the bull. The other is directly in front of the creature, apparently gripping a horn under her armpit; and the boy seems to be in the middle of a flying somersault over its back.

The assembled evidence told Evans the whole story. A pair of exquisitely worked gold cups from Vaphio in Greece but obviously of Cretan manufacture showed a group of boys and girls capturing bulls in nets or with the aid of a decoy cow. A crude terracotta group from Koumasa in Crete consisted of a big clumsy bull with a tiny human figure clinging to each

One of the finest and most expressive pieces of miniature art from Crete is a small bronze group consisting of a powerful bull with a young acrobat, connected to the bull only by the locks of his streaming hair, flying over its head in the perilous back somersault which was the object of this dangerous sport. The piece is incomplete in some of the details where the bronze has failed to flow, but it is still a brilliant testimonial to the artist's feeling for vitality and movement. British Museum, London.

opposite The Cretan ritual sport which may have provided the foundations of the minotaur legend is depicted on a fresco, much damaged and questionably restored, from a small court in the east wing of the palace of Knossos. A heavy, short-legged bull charges a group of young male and female acrobats who are all dressed alike in scanty male garb, and while the girls distract the animal's attention or provide a steadying hand to help the performer away, the boy throws a back somersault over the bull's head.

work at Knossos. We do not know the exact nature of the political system which raised the Bronze Age Cretans to such heights, but whatever it was, its heart was the palace, which wielded such great power that when it finally collapsed and disappeared it passed into Greek legend under its Minoan name: the Labyrinth. The original meaning of the word is simple and devoid of sinister or supernatural implications. One of the commonest symbols of Minoan religion was an axe with a curved blade on either side of the handle. Paintings, models and other representations of this cult object were found in profusion all over Knossos, and the ancient word for the double axe was *labrys*. 'Labyrinth' therefore only meant 'House of the Double Axe'; but it is easy to see how, in the minds of the Bronze Age Greek visitors to Crete, it lost its meaning and came to signify 'maze'. Living as they did at that time in tiny two-roomed houses, they must have reacted with awestricken bewilderment to the Labyrinth, with its trackless networks of corridors, halls, stairs, courts and shrines, storey piled on storey from the dank underground cellars to the shining roof crowned with a coping of huge stylised bull's horns.

The image of the bull was everywhere at Knossos; massive beasts were depicted on frescoes and carved gems, far larger than life-size in proportions to the puny human figures shown alongside them. The further Evans's

horn and another swarming up its head. A slender ivory and gold figurine of a boy with raised arms, who seems from his intense expression to be awaiting some ordeal, was dressed like the frescoed bull leapers. Numerous carved gems showed a charging bull with a human figure in flight over its head, and a steatite rhyton was carved in low relief with a similar scene, except that here the bull was victorious and its adversary was crumpled helplessly over the flailing horns. One of the clearest representations was a magnificent bronze of a bull and an acrobat. It may have been a foundry reject, as the metal has failed to flow into some parts of the mould. These, unfortunately, include the acrobat's hands and arms, which might have provided useful evidence about this puzzling activity.

Basing his conclusions on these objects, Evans tried to reconstruct the sequence of events. The young acrobats, he believed, brought the captive bull to a suitable arena. They provoked it to charge them and, just before the moment of impact, grasped its horns. Using the impetus of the bull's charge and toss to help them, they flung themselves up into the air and somersaulted to land on its back, finishing by springing away with the assistance

left The prevalence of the bull motif in Cretan art is one of its most striking characteristics, and perhaps suggests the importance of the animal in the ancient religious cult. The magnificent rhyton, or pouring vessel, from the Little Palace at Knossos is carved in black serpentine stone and has goldplated horns and inlaid eyes of crystal and shell which give it a disturbingly life-like stare. (The horns are a modern restoration.) The sculptor has conveyed with consummate artistry both the power and dignity of the sacred animal.
Archaeological Museum, Heraklion.

Almost as frequent in Cretan art as the bull theme is the double-axe motif. It is one of the most persistent subjects, and appears almost everywhere, from flimsy gold miniatures of obvious votive function through a whole range of everyday artifacts such as this large storage jar of the late Minoan period decorated with ritual axes and stylised plants. Archaeological Museum, Heraklion.

of the catcher who waited behind to steady them as they landed. Evans could find no other explanation which fitted all the representations; but such a feat seemed so foolhardy that no one in their right mind would attempt it, and if they did, the results must surely be fatal. He took his doubts to an American rodeo expert, who confirmed them by declaring that the bull-leap shown in the Minoan painting was impossible. An angry bull, he learned, does not gore and toss frontally, but with a sideways movement of the head which brings its whole weight into play behind one horn. The acrobat would need a steady, even thrust at take-off to carry him over on to the bull's back, and he could not possibly get this from the normal movement of an attacking bull, which would twist its head sideways and shake it violently on impact. However, despite these objections, the combined evidence of Cretan art could not be gainsaid, and Evans was finally compelled to accept that, given a confined space and a clumsy, short-legged bull trained to docility as far as such training is practicable, an occasional acrobat succeeded in performing this fantastic stunt, whatever the experts might say.

Evans was never able completely to dispel his own very reasonable doubts; but later researchers have produced some modifications to his original theory which help to bring it well within the bounds of possibility. In 1965 Professor O. Lendle offered a new explanation of the bull-leap. He suggested that the chief acrobat never actually touched the bull's head at all, but achieved his leap with the help of two girl assistants whose role was to grab the horns from behind on either side, thus holding the beast's head down and distracting its attention at this most critical moment. This time there was no need to speculate about whether or not the feat was possible, for a contemporary version is, in fact, still in existence. In south-western France a form of the bull-sport is still played in which the leading performer faces a charging animal head-on and then throws a mighty somersault over its head, landing behind it. In this case, too, the animal's head is held down, but a rope halter takes the place of the two girls who assisted the Minoan star acrobat.

If this explains how the bull-leap was done, the last remaining doubt was settled by Professor J. Graham, a leading expert on Cretan architecture, who was able to identify the confined space which would have made the bull's charge so much less lethal. He showed that the buildings abutting on the central courtyard of the palace have provision for gates and palisades where there is no structural necessity for a barrier of this description. At Mallia post-holes for the installation of a temporary hurdle still survive in the spaces of the main colonnade, and

since the distance between them is too large to keep a Minoan out of the court, they were perhaps intended to pen a much larger creature into it. Such an arrangement would provide both a magnificent grandstand view for the spectators and an easily available place of refuge for a hard-pressed performer. From this (and a convincing array of supporting evidence) he deduced that the bull games took place in the courtyard which lay in the heart of the Labyrinth.

In the study of Cretan civilisation, excavation and scholarly interpretation have worked together from the beginning. Evans's investigations at Knossos did more than reveal a brilliant and hitherto unknown culture; they demonstrated once again the unwisdom of turning a deaf ear to the voice of ancient tradition. Theseus himself is lost in the mists of Bronze Age antiquity, but the Labyrinth was proved to be a sober historical fact, and was shown to have been the scene of desperately perilous, often fatal encounters with a monstrous bull. Even the specific and superficially unlikely detail of the legend which has maidens as well as youths engaged in this deadly sport has been confirmed.

In the face of these facts, it is clear that the tellers of old wives' tales and sailors' yarns were wiser than they realised when they related the story of the Bull of Minos and the Labyrinth.

A procession of shouting and singing farmers, radiating vitality and high spirits, is the subject of this stone vase (detail) from Haghia Triada. Such objects, which throw light on the customs and way of life of ordinary people, are in many ways more valuable to archaeology than the art of the great palaces, which only reveals the life-style of a small segment of the community – the very rich.

Pompeii and Herculaneum

In 1860 the kingdom of Naples officially became part of the new Italy, and shortly after this an archaeologist named Fiorelli was appointed director of the excavations at Pompeii. It was a plum job; probably the most distinguished post in the archaeological world of his day, but as he surveyed the task before him his emotions must sometimes have bordered on despair. The site was huge; he was not called upon simply to disengage a temple, palace or fortress, or even a small settlement, but a whole city and all its outworks and ramifications. He was not dealing with sturdy time-worn stone walls which had survived the centuries intact, but often with incredibly fragile organic material such as wood, vegetable matter, papyrus and even fabric which could crumble at the lightest touch and for which the embryonic science of the time had no answer. Anyone might have been forgiven for feeling over-awed by the responsibility for this wonderful site where the daily life of the Romans lay preserved like a fly in amber beneath a blanket of volcanic ash and clay, the only one of its kind and therefore of unique and unparalleled importance. These factors would no doubt have made Fiorelli's job a challenge, but there were others which must have turned it into something like a nightmare.

If he could have started from scratch the problem would have been relatively simple, but for more than a century Pompeii had been subject to 'investigations' ranging from the desultory burrowings of individual looters to concerted assaults by teams of sappers, all ostensibly operating under the banner of Archaeology and all pursuing a single object: the rapacious plunder of ancient works of art.

The discovery of this seemingly inexhaustible treasure house was an offshoot of the earlier excavations at neighbouring Herculaneum which in their turn had resulted from a practical application of academic studies. Long before the sites had been located, scholars had been aware that there were at least two buried cities close to Vesuvius if only they knew where to dig. Several classical authorities mentioned the appalling eruption of AD 79 which buried Pompeii, Herculaneum and Stabiae, causing such destruction that no serious attempt at salvage or rebuilding was ever thought worthwhile. One of these texts is the nearest possible thing to an eye-witness account, for at the time of the eruption the younger Pliny was staying at Misenum on the northern arm of the Bay of Naples in the home of his uncle, a distinguished naturalist, writer and admiral of the imperial fleet, who lost his life helping to evacuate refugees from the stricken towns. The great historian Tacitus asked Pliny for a description of these events and the answering letter, based on personal observation and the stories told by the surviving members of his uncle's party, still exists. Young Pliny's letter supplements the material evidence to provide a detailed picture of the day the world ended for the cities under the volcano.

Towards the end of August in AD 79 the people of this beautiful and prosperous region were celebrating one of their many religious festivals. There was no warning, apart from a few earth tremors, but this had happened before and was not regarded with any great alarm. The inhabitants did not realise that these earthquakes were caused by a build-up of pressure inside the mountain, for they had no idea that their cities lay among the foothills of an active volcano. The geographer Strabo had noted that the rocks showed traces of volcanic origin, but no signs of life had been seen within recorded memory and in the 1st century AD Vesuvius was a fertile peak, thickly overgrown right up to the summit with timber and vines, and famous for its profusion of game. These centuries of quiescence served to augment the ferocity of the eruption, for during the dormant years an unusually thick crust had formed, closing off all the minor vents and blow-holes which might otherwise have helped to keep pressure down and requiring a peculiar degree of violence to break through it.

By a grim irony one of the festivals being celebrated that August was intended to allow the denizens of the underworld to emerge. Seldom in the history of ritual can a ceremony have been more hideously successful. Without

opposite The palaestra, or sports ground, of Herculaneum was unusually large for so small a town. A colonnade surrounded an open space where the young athletes practised their skills, and around it were changing rooms, a meeting hall and a swimming bath. In Greek as well as Roman towns the palaestra was as much a social as an athletic centre.

any preliminaries of mushroom cloud or fire the mountain emitted a roar and split in two, hurling up a jet of superheated steam, white-hot rocks, poisonous gases and countless tons of volcanic ash and stones. The brilliant light of a Campanian midsummer day was totally blotted out by the ash cloud, and from the black sky, torn by sheets of lightning and gouts of flame from the crater, the lethal detritus of the explosion smashed down on the settlements along the bay. In a few hours everything which had not been overthrown or burned was buried deep under a thick layer of scalding ash and pumice.

Since the wind was blowing from the north at the time, most of this destruction fell on the cities to the south of the volcano. The thriving little seaport of Herculaneum, which lay even closer to the western slopes, was overtaken by a different fate. One of the side-effects of the heat emerging from the crater was a freak rainstorm which lashed the white-hot ash into an avalanche of boiling mud and sent it rolling down over Herculaneum. The people were, in one respect, luckier than those of Pompeii. Their

danger was so much more obvious and imminent that they dropped everything and fled. When a mountain is being torn apart immediately overhead and a seething wall of mud several metres high is bearing down on your home you do not stop to take the bread out of the oven or to drink the wine in your cup, or even to collect your valuables, and in consequence most of the citizens of Herculaneum were saved.

The Pompeians, farther from Vesuvius and under no direct threat from the lava flow, did not act so promptly, and though the majority escaped, at least 2000 left it too late. A number of them tried to shelter from the falling ash and rocks in cellars: a fatal choice, for the poisonous fumes of sulphur and hydrochloric acid rapidly filled these low-lying places, annihilating every living thing. Others, like the priests of Isis, stayed too long collecting their treasures; they were killed by falling columns as they hurried through the Forum towards the gate farthest from the mountain. Many more must have been overcome and vanished without trace in the open country beyond the city walls as the people fled as best they could.

The government passed a few half-hearted measures for the relief of the survivors, but none of the buried towns was economically or strategically important enough to warrant the expenses and difficulties of rebuilding. Besides, the mountain was still smoking and grumbling ominously enough to discourage immediate re-settlement (it has never been completely dormant again). As the years passed the mud smothering Herculaneum petrified into stone and the ash-blanket over Pompeii hardened, earth accumulated above them and in time even the location of the cities was forgotten. The shore line shifted, the town of Resina was built over Herculaneum and farms and villages covered Pompeii. Only the peasants who farmed the region preserved some dim folk memory of former significance for they called the Pompeii district La Cività; but they did not know why.

From the Renaissance onwards classical remains turned up in significant quantities to the south and west of Vesuvius, but no serious attempts were made to locate the lost cities until the early 18th century. At this time the Bay of Naples was part of the Habsburg empire, and an Austrian nobleman, the Prince d'Elboeuf, decided that classical scholarship suggested his estate at Portici as a promising excavation site. He assembled a small army of workmen and set them to boring shafts here and there in the lava rock. Unfortunately for the future of archaeology, one of his earliest attempts lighted on the theatre of Herculaneum–'unfortunately' because his sole idea, like that of many of his successors, was to find treasures and works of

Archaeological wish-fulfilment: an early print shows an immaculately dressed gentleman reclining negligently at his ease reading a manuscript while at his feet a group of suitably picturesque workmen, rummaging barely a metre below ground level, unearth basketsful of miraculously intact finds. In the background Vesuvius supplies an appropriately romantic atmosphere with its plume of smoke.

art. Houses and other architectural remains he regarded as so much rubbish blocking up the excavation and obstructing its real purpose, to be demolished without record and shovelled out of the way. After some seven years of these smash-and-grab tactics Naples passed to the control of the Spanish Bourbons and the tunnels were abandoned until 1738. King Carlos III then decided to take an interest in the project, and since the problem was one of digging and boring, it seemed appropriate to the authorities to place a colonel in the Engineers in charge of the work. Of Rocco Alcubierre it could fairly be said that his methods were less destructive to the site than those of the Prince d'Elboeuf, but not much less.

Supervising a gang of convict labourers, Alcubierre extended the original tunnels in the theatre and constructed others, but by 1748 he was beginning to think that the problem of driving galleries through the solid rock was greater than the results warranted. What is more, although 17 centuries had passed since the eruption, its destructive power was not yet completely expended, for the volcanic material

Johann Joseph Winckelmann (1717–68) was among the first classical scholars to think of classifying ancient art by attempting to put it into its chronological and historical context. Passionately devoted to the spirit of Hellenism, his influence on scholarship was profound, and from his day onwards the dilettantism of earlier times was gradually replaced by a more serious professional approach.

Although Herculaneum was discovered some years before Pompeii, the much easier excavating conditions caused earlier excavators to concentrate on the latter site. At first their sole aim was treasure or works of art, but the 19th-century teams shown here were already beginning to pay serious attention to the reconstruction of the surviving remains.

As the Roman empire expanded, troops, colonists, merchants and administrators travelled widely and came in contact with many exotic cults which gradually began to take root in Italy alongside the 'official' religion of the Olympian gods. The 'mystery' rites of the Egyptian goddess Isis had a particularly strong appeal, and a temple in her honour was found in Pompeii.

The Villa of the Mysteries, just outside the northern
gate of Pompeii, contained a room frescoed entirely
with strange scenes of a cult initiation ceremony,
executed in brilliant colours on a scarlet background.
The exact nature of the ritual is unknown, but a
curiously exotic, even perverse, atmosphere pervades
as the initiant undergoes stages of the rite.

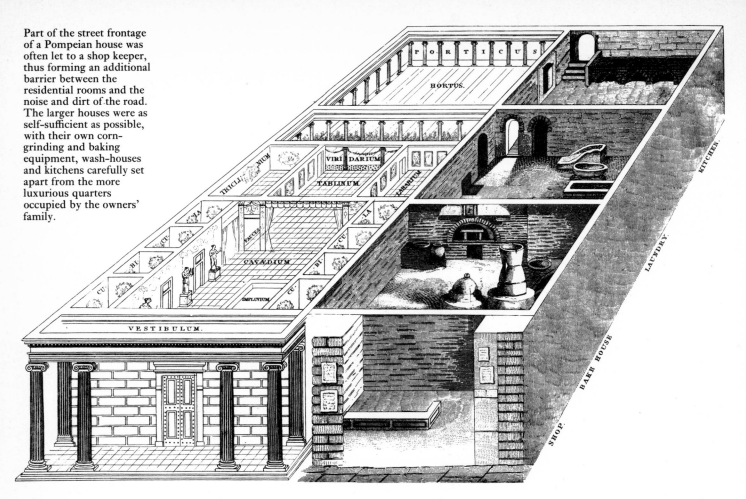

Part of the street frontage of a Pompeian house was often let to a shop keeper, thus forming an additional barrier between the residential rooms and the noise and dirt of the road. The larger houses were as self-sufficient as possible, with their own corn-grinding and baking equipment, wash-houses and kitchens carefully set apart from the more luxurious quarters occupied by the owners' family.

of the passages was oozing sulphurous vapours which could be highly dangerous. He decided to look for an easier and more rewarding site and directed his work forces to the district of Torre Annunziata. Almost at once he struck a large wall painting and the skeleton of one of the eruption's many victims. Fifteen years passed before his new discovery was identified, but in fact he had found Pompeii.

For the next few years, however, he made only half-hearted attempts to exploit the new site. It was far easier than Herculaneum to excavate and less dangerous, but it was correspondingly less productive. The boiling mud which engulfed the sea port had acted as a soft pervasive blanket which sealed everything in the city and preserved even the most perishable material, but the tons of white-hot rocks and ash which rained down on Pompeii had crushed many buildings and set fire to others. The excavators dug a few random areas which they did not even trouble to record, and then turned back for the time being to the richer pickings at Herculaneum.

Here they brought to light a palaestra and a magnificent villa which housed not only a rich citizen's unrivalled sculpture collection but an exhaustive library of papyrus texts. Each one still lay in its place on the shelves, contained in a wooden box, but when they were opened and eager scholars tried to unroll the texts, they crumbled and collapsed into ashes. The occasion, however, produced the right man. One of the curators of the Vatican Library at that time was the Jesuit Father Biaggio, who had an outstanding talent for deciphering and copying even the dimmest and most obscure writings. He constructed a frame strung with threads into which the scrolls were fed a millimetre at a time as they were unrolled, a backing of paste and gold-beater's skin supplying the necessary body. With limitless patience and skill he succeeded in rescuing and transcribing many of the texts, only to find that they were nearly all undistinguished Epicurean philosophical essays. It was a poor reward for his labour, but at least he had tried to establish the need for careful preservation and recording of the finds.

Alcubierre's excavations were attracting scholars' attention from all over Europe. A body of scholars, the Academy of Herculaneum (later to be extended and known as the Academy of Sciences and Fine Arts of Naples) was founded to study and publish the discoveries and to direct the investigations, and among the sightseers who converged on the rediscovered cities was Johann Winckelmann. His work was to earn him the name 'father of archaeology', since he was the first scholar to form deductions about ancient life from the surviving artifacts. An engaging mixture of scholar and scamp, he was an Austrian who had always been devoted to the classics. Settling in Rome to conduct his studies on the spot, he soon found that there was very little future for a Protestant in the Vatican, so he promptly accepted the Catholic faith and was appointed librarian to Cardinal Passionei.

When he came to Herculaneum it did not take him long to quarrel with Alcubierre. He was horrified by the wholesale wreckage of ancient artifacts, and registered a vigorous protest when he saw a bronze inscription being torn letter by letter from its mountings and tumbled indiscriminately into a basket. Even worse was the destruction of a superb bronze quadriga from the theatre which was so badly knocked about that only a single horse could be reconstructed from the scattered fragments. Despite his concern for these relics, even Winckelmann had no interest to spare for the houses. When Alcubierre's Swiss assistant Charles Weber tentatively suggested that the town should be methodically cleared and examined, scorn was poured on the idea. What possible point could there be, Winkelmann demanded, in wasting time and money in 'laying bare a parcel of old ruinous walls, merely to satisfy the ill-judged curiosity of some virtuosi'?

Sporadic discoveries on both sites continued to delight the cognoscenti, each building being methodically stripped of its contents before it was used as a dumping ground for the debris from the next. Everything movable was taken to Naples, and even the frescoes, which might reasonably be considered fixtures, were cut away from the walls, often to be distributed as diplomatic or personal gifts around the courts of Europe. With the establishment of the Napoleonic régime archaeological activity received a powerful stimulus from Joseph Bonaparte and his successor, Joachim Murat, husband of the emperor's sister Caroline, whose

opposite bottom On passing through the street door the first room one entered in most Pompeian houses was the atrium, a roughly square hall surrounded by smaller rooms. Its only light and ventilation came from a square opening in the middle of the roof immediately below which was a shallow pool to catch rain-water, known as the impluvium. In the ruined House of Cornelius the impluvium is seen in the foreground, while beyond the atrium is the courtyard garden.

The Forum at Pompeii was at once a civic, commercial and religious centre, and one of the chief gathering places of the citizens for casual social contacts. The offices of the town's administrators stood around the open space where market goods were set out for sale, and at one end was the temple of Apollo, the city's patron god.

interested presence at the dig is noted in several of the scanty and erratic records. In terms of manpower these were the great days of excavation, with up to 700 workers and 20 carts being employed at any one time on clearing the tombs, the amphitheatre and the forum of Pompeii.

The political instability which afflicted Italy for many years after the fall of Napoleon did not encourage archaeological advance. The excavations were continued intermittently, but little was achieved in the way of tangible progress. However, as the 19th century advanced, a new attitude towards archaeology became increasingly apparent and experts in charge of the investigation of Pompeii began to awake for the first time to the fact that the site had more to offer than an endless supply of *objets d'art*. The prevailing political climate of Europe fostered the novel idea that the ancient world did not consist exclusively of heroic statesmen, writers and artists but of ordinary people who worked, loved, lived and died very much as men have always done in every age including our own. Scholars now understood the importance of exploring and preserving the city as a whole and trying to interpret its unique evidence on the daily lives of the Romans, and this approach, far from detracting from the status of archaeology, gave it a poignancy and relevance it had never achieved in its 'aristocratic' phase. Everything except the current circumstances seemed ready for a major breakthrough. Then came the 1860s, the affiliation of Naples and the appointment of Fiorelli.

Examining the battered site and the huge mass of chaotic notes and diaries, most of which were so vague and inaccurate that he could not tell which building they referred to, Fiorelli set about introducing some kind of system and order into past records and future proceedings.

It seemed desirable to begin by establishing the exact dimensions of the site, since the most recent map transpired to be more than half a century out of date. Accordingly he set his team to following the line of the city walls and carefully noting the position of the various gates. Another urgent problem which had to be tackled simultaneously was that of drainage. Earlier excavators, avidly rummaging for treasures, had overlooked the fact that once the earth is removed from any part of a site it is inevitably exposed to all kinds of weather, and the spring and autumn rain in Campania can be fierce. The scattered diggings must have become pits full of water twice a year, and the damage to fragile ancient remains cannot be assessed. Water conduits were cleared and a new era in the investigation of Pompeii was inaugurated.

Once the line of the enclosing walls had been traced it was not difficult to establish the main topography of the city. It proved to have been designed (with occasional slight variations) on the rational grid system associated with the Greek Hippodamus of Miletus, with straight roads dividing the area into more or less rectangular blocks. Using the streets as a basis Fiorelli marked out the site into districts, which were then subdivided into blocks and buildings, each being numbered for easy reference. By applying this system every detail of the excavation could always be easily identified and located and each find pinpointed and described with absolute accuracy. Apart from a few necessary modifications Fiorelli's numbered grid is still in use today.

If part of his aim was to present the everyday Roman of the 1st century to the scholars of the 19th, he succeeded dramatically in one respect. During the course of the dig he noticed a curious configuration in the hardened ash in several places, and on closer examination he

As the choking ash and sulphur fumes from the eruption fell about the citizens of Pompeii, they died almost immediately. The ash hardened around the bodies and, as each corpse disintegrated, a hollow 'mould' was left. When this hollow was injected with wet plaster a perfect cast of the unfortunate person at the moment of his death was obtained. This method is now being used for other perishable organic materials, and many long-vanished objects can be reproduced in plaster casts with absolute fidelity.

was able to deduce what had happened. The Pompeians who had died lay where they fell and the hot volcanic ash covered them, seeping in and enfolding every detail of garments, features and even hair. In time the bodies vanished, but the solidified ash stayed in place, forming a perfect 'mould' of the long-dead Roman, and by injecting wet plaster into these hollows Fiorelli was able to reconstruct with grim accuracy their appearance at the moment of death. The beggar almost naked except for a pair of smart new shoes, the mother trying vainly to shelter her little daughter in her arms, a number of wretched slaves left behind to guard property which no one was ever to reclaim, the prisoner shackled in the gaol, the gladiators in their barracks and the watchdog struggling frantically to free himself from his chain as the ash rose round him; they and hundreds like them have been reconstructed and their pallid plaster ghosts are to be seen in the site museum. This is no place for the soft-hearted. Indeed, one cannot avoid the thought that there is something revolting in exhibiting the last agonies of these tragic creatures for the titillation of sensation-hunting tourists. But if archaeology is about people and

It must have been a highly opulent citizen who owned the House of the Faun, one of the largest and most complex in Pompeii, which occupies a whole city block and boasts not one but two peristyle gardens. It is named from the dancing bronze figure, so full of vitality and *joie de vivre*, which stands in the middle of the impluvium, and would be the first sight to greet visitors as they entered.

Pompeii had a large proportion of well-to-do citizens whose full and active social lives included lavish dinner parties. An enormous variety of dishes were served, as the Romans were keen connoisseurs of exotic and fine food, but the kitchens from which these culinary masterpieces emerged were often cramped and sparsely equipped, like that of the House of the Vetii. With plentiful slave labour available, the rich paid little consideration to the comfort or convenience of their servants.

its function is to serve the truth, then even the dead have much to tell the living.

Fiorelli had his work cut out in ascertaining the layout of the site and clearing up the muddled records of past operations, but his successors Ruggiero, de Petra and Sogliano were able to make rapid progress. Their aim was to restore each building as nearly as possible to its original appearance by replacing roofs, setting up fallen columns and re-laying mosaics, all the furniture and decorations which had survived being left in place. These restorations provoked another outburst of the controversy which has existed almost since the beginning of serious archaeology. The strict purists believe that earth and debris should be removed from a site but it should otherwise be left exactly as it is found; their opponents think that every possible structure should be restored and missing portions extensively replaced. Both views have something to recommend them as well as substantial drawbacks. There is, perhaps, more danger in over-enthusiastic restoration than in letting well alone, as personal views which are not always properly supported by evidence can result in a site which belongs far more to the period of the restorer than to that of the original builder. The best course lies, as usual, in

moderation and a discriminating application of some aspects of both methods.

Restoration techniques aided by up-to-date laboratory science have been outstandingly successful at Pompeii, and some of the houses now evoke a vivid picture of the life style of its citizens in the first century. To discuss the 'Pompeian house' can be misleading as no two of them are exactly alike, but a number of common features indicate the architectural principles on which they were planned. The city appears to have had two parallel streams of activity: the lively, noisy, dirty, smelly and frequently ribald business of the streets which

was energetically conducted in the shops, road-ways, public buildings and open spaces, and the secluded life of the private homes. These were designed with the idea of excluding the uproar of the roads and supplying adequate protection from the heat. Given that hardly any window glass was available (a major limitation of domestic comfort) the Pompeian architect produced one of the nost successful hot-climate town houses of all time. He was fortunate in having plenty of space available, and he made full use of it in his admirable solution to the problem of urban living.

The house had two main focal points: the atrium and the garden. The first of these was a large, roughly square room reached directly from the entrance. It was surrounded by smaller rooms giving on to it, sometimes with a loggia providing access to an upper storey, and its most imaginative feature was the impluvium, a square opening in the middle of the roof below which was a shallow flat-bottomed pool of the same shape and size. This aperture supplied light and ventilation without the necessity of breaching the walls on to the street while the pool must have kept the air pleasantly cool and fresh. The walls might be painted in imitation of marble veneer, frescoed or covered with colourful pictorial mosaics, and the floor also boasted a mosaic pavement, usually a simple and severely restrained design carried out in black and white.

Among the rooms beyond the atrium was a small domestic shrine containing the house-hold's ancestral gods and the tablinium, the private room of the master and mistress of the house. Passing through this complex one came to perhaps the most attractive part of the build-ing: a charming courtyard garden surrounded by a colonnade on to which all the rest of the rooms opened. Thus all the rooms on the ground floor overlooked either the garden or the atrium rather than the street, and none of them was exposed to direct sunshine. For those who en-joyed watching and participating in the com-munal life of the streets which has always been such a conspicuous feature of Italian towns, there were balconies on the first floor, but apart from these the interior was as private as any country villa.

A great deal of artistry was expended on the gardens. By minute study of carbonised remains and of the holes in the ground left by roots, experts have been able to identify the plants which were grown, and some of the gardens have been replanted. The Romans did not believe in keeping the kitchen garden separate from the flowers, and a charming mixture of shrubs, blossoms, aromatic herbs and vegetables was grown around the statues of divinities, pools, fountains, cages of singing birds and theatrical actors' masks which combined to

One of the larger reception rooms in the House of the Vetii shows the variety of painted decoration used in Roman interiors. Panels of variegated stone alternate with *trompe l'oeil* architectural fea-tures, and in a prominent position on each wall is an important painting. That on the left, for instance, shows Pasiphaë, wife of King Minos of Crete, with the inventor Daedalus and the hollow wooden cow which enabled her to mate with a sacred bull and become the mother of the Minotaur.

below One of the most spectacular rooms in the House of the Vetii at Pompeii is decorated with an important painting in the middle of each wall depicting scenes from the legend of Theseus and the Minotaur. The episode shown in this panel occurs immediately after the defeat of the monster. Theseus, following the trail of thread, has retraced his steps to the entrance of the Labyrinth (firmly located as Roman by its arched doorway), dragging the corpse after him. He is awaited by his followers, who greet him with relief while they instinctively shrink from the dead Minotaur.

bottom An elegant couch from Pompeii is made of dark wood lavishly gilded and equipped with a matching footstool. This piece shows clearly how much these excavations influenced current fashions – in the late 18th and early 19th centuries furnishings in the classical style were reproduced for exclusive drawing-rooms all over Europe.

right see page 44.

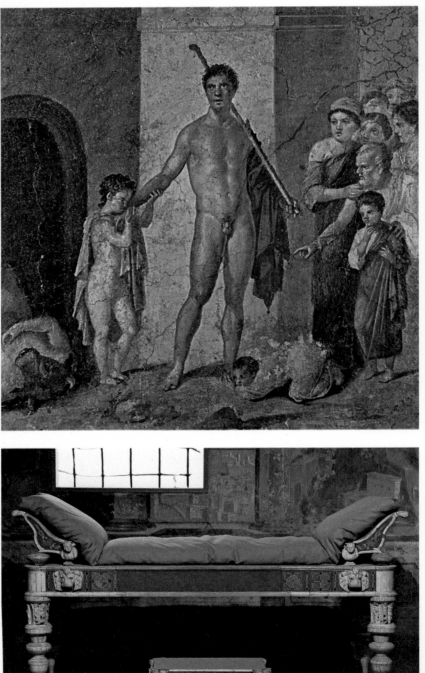

delight all the senses simultaneously.

It is curious to find that though the Romans employed so much ingenuity in laying on the necessary plumbing for their garden fountains they were very much less concerned about their domestic water supplies. All the homes had a kitchen, some had a bathroom and a few had a lavatory, but for the most part they were hopelessly inadequate. The last refinements of luxurious bathing were provided by the public baths, but private bathrooms were comparatively makeshift affairs. The same was true of lavatories; a splendid public establishment had a long marble bench with holes at companionable intervals along it, but in the citizens' houses the latrine was usually a primitive fixture in a dark and cramped cupboard under the stairs or far too near the kitchen. This in its turn was a surprisingly tiny and ill-equipped room in view of the Romans' sophisticated tastes in cookery.

The restorers achieved remarkable results at Pompeii but at Herculaneum their services were scarcely required at all. Sealed in an airtight mass of solid rock, even the most perishable materials had neither burnt nor decomposed, and though the utmost care had to be employed to preserve these delicate fabrics once they were exposed to the air again, by this time archaeological science was fully equipped to meet the problem.

Throughout the 19th century Herculaneum had been largely ignored apart from two short spells of intense activity, but in 1927 the dig was finally and permanently reopened under the brilliant direction of Professor Maiuri, who was appointed in 1924 and conducted the excavations for nearly 40 years. The dank, forbidding shafts and tunnels of the earlier investigations were abandoned (they still exist, but are not open to the public), and slowly but steadily the layer of rock, more than 30 metres thick in places, was stripped away to reveal the city. It was a labour of Herculean proportions, but the rewards were commensurate. The shops were still stocked with merchandise, elegant furniture with spindly cabriole legs was found in the living rooms, and cooking pots stood on the kitchen stoves. In one eerie case a citizen had

fled leaving his lunch unfinished, and the fruit and cakes still lay on the dining-room table. The visitor to the upper floors in Herculaneum does not climb a modern reconstruction but the original Roman staircase, the woodwork protected only by the addition of plate-glass covers to the treads. None of the finds are removed from the site unless they are too valuable or too fragile to be left at the mercy of the public and the elements.

In 1872 Fiorelli estimated that the next 60 years would see the entire excavation completed and published. Today two-fifths of Pompeii and more than half Herculaneum are still buried, although the work has continued with very little interruption since Fiorelli's time. Progressive improvements in archaeological methods dictate a far slower pace of operating. Former excavators used pick-axes or even blasting powder. Contemporary experts may start off with electric drills and mechanical shovels, but they are more likely to finish each section of the dig with a fine brush, and every discovery has to be recorded and photographed in position so that if it should disintegrate when moved it will not be completely lost to scholarship. The fragments of crushed buildings are repaired and put back into place as they come to light where once the whole area was cleared before any restorations were attempted, so that a great deal was left to chance or imagination when the time came. Even the imprint of decomposed fibres is carefully noted and casts taken so that an exact semblance of the original can be put in its place. Progress is slow and will be slower as more advanced methods evolve, but year by year as the excavations progress increasing light is thrown on the ordinary Roman people and the reality of their lives.

Such works as the Colosseum and Pantheon, the poems of Virgil and the histories of Livy are among the major monuments of Roman civilisation; but great artists are necessarily set apart from the rank and file of the people, and their productions tell us very little about the thoughts, beliefs and customs of the man in the street. This is the gap which is so satisfyingly filled by Pompeii and Herculaneum. A few representative graffiti tell us more than any leading work of literature about what the Romans thought was a good joke or a good insult, an enjoyable experience or a bad bargain, a fine dinner or a poor night's lodging and what was really significant to them in the trivia of personal relationships as well as the major issues of politics and religion. A well-preserved house in Herculaneum is more illustrative of everyday living conditions and habits than all the grandiose official sculptures of the Ara Pacis or Trajan's Column.

When an ancient site is abandoned it is usually for one of two reasons: either the people decide of their own free will to move elsewhere or it is devastated as a result of enemy action. In both cases there is nothing to stop the inhabitants or the conquerors from taking away almost everything except the bare walls and roofs of the buildings before the earth and debris of the centuries begins to move in, and only the skeleton of what was once a living town is left for future archaeologists to disinter. But Pompeii and Herculaneum were neither left to gradual dereliction nor looted. When the volcano erupted in AD 79 all the life which had been in full swing right up to that moment was seized and held in suspension instantly, permanently and completely, like the mastodon which was preserved in the Russian permafrost. Gradually the cities are being revived, and no one can doubt that each new phase of the excavation will produce fresh revelations; great monuments of art will come to light as well as the minor but no less valuable treasures of knowledge about the ordinary people who lived in the cities on the foothills of Vesuvius.

With both security and quietness in mind, town houses were designed to have as few openings as possible giving on to the street, since there was virtually no glass for windows. Entry was usually by means of a single door which was presided over by a porter in a small room beside it. This watchman was, in several cases, supplemented by an equally fearsome canine guardian whose presence was made known by the warning *cave canem* ('beware of the dog') in mosaic on the floor, accompanied by a lively picture of the animal for the benefit of those who could not read.

CAVE CANEM

The Rosetta Stone deciphered

Ancient Egypt might justifiably be characterised as primarily a culture of graffiti. Seldom in the course of history can there have been a people so persistently devoted as the Egyptians to writing on walls, nor one who raised the practice to such a fine art. Obsessed as they were with ideas of immortality and eternity, each generation strove to perpetuate their own names and deeds for all time in some way which would not be at the mercy of the kind of mischance that can wipe out all living witnesses to the memory of a man's greatness, or even his existence. In order to achieve this they developed written characters of matchless sculptural clarity with which they covered all their buildings and monuments from floor to ceiling.

Egyptian archaeology was never faced with the problems besetting the rediscovery of a lost site or civilisation, for even the most short-sighted or indifferent traveller could scarcely remain unaware of the pyramids, the sphinx and the temples of Luxor and Karnak. They were already well known as tourist attractions and a source of mysterious fascination to the classical Greeks, who scribbled their names on the ancient stones with all the assiduity of their modern counterparts. The hot, dry air of Egypt provides conditions which are particularly favourable to the survival of most materials, and scarcely any early people left such abundant remains, not only of their temples, tombs and public works, but their furniture, equipment, jewels, clothes and even their own bodies, ritually preserved against the resurrection day. Nearly every item in this unparalleled wealth of material was inscribed with exquisite written symbols; the authentic voice of ancient Egypt was perpetuated in the hieroglyphs. But nobody could read them.

Over the centuries many people had tried, their approaches ranging from serious academic studies to the wilder flights of the lunatic fringe. Typical of these curiosities was the book by Athanasius Kircher, a German Jesuit scholar living in Rome in the 17th century. After a distinguished career as a teacher of mathematics, philosophy and Oriental languages, Kircher turned to the problem of the hieroglyphs, and in 1643 he published *Lingua Aegyptiaca*. This erudite Latin work offered a full decipherment complete with systematic grammar and vocabulary. Its only drawback was that it proceeded directly from Kircher's imagination without any reference whatever to facts or reality.

Few if any scholars thought to study the problem at its source. In those days Egypt was distant, dangerous and strange, and at a time when most of Europe believed all possible human virtues could exist only within the framework of Christianity, Egypt was simply un-Christian. It was not until the end of the 18th century that Napoleon's invasion of North Africa brought Egypt into the headlines of the war news and Egyptian antiquities into the forefront of fashion. Napoleon had a shrewd grasp of the importance of propaganda and international prestige, so in addition to his army he took with him a body of scholars, draughtsmen and scientists. While the artillery used the monuments for target practice whenever they had nothing better to do, the intrepid savants scrambled along in the wake of the army studying, measuring, drawing, describing and collecting antiquities, their enthusiasm undimmed by the appalling conditions under which they often had to work. Napoleon himself soon returned to France, and Nelson's victory at the Battle of the Nile put an end to French hopes of eastern conquest, but the flood of information about ancient Egypt which reached Europe with the returning scholars gave rise to widespread and continually expanding interest in that mysterious civilisation. Modish ladies draped in what they hoped were classical muslins posed on ebony and gold chairs with lion feet and sphinx arm-terminals while antiquarians applied themselves afresh to the problems of the hieroglyphs, for this time they had reasonable hopes of success.

In August 1799 a squad of French soldiers had been repairing an outpost named Fort St Julien at Rosetta (Rashid) near Alexandria. Stone is scarce in the delta and every available piece had to be pressed into service. The Rosetta Stone might easily have been broken up

opposite The hypostyle hall of the great temple complex at Karnak now lies open to the sky, but it was once a dark and claustrophobic forest of thick, heavy columns, close-set in the dim interior. Shafts, capitals and roof beams are entirely covered with carved figures and signs as generations of kings made their bid for immortality.

or hopelessly defaced to fill in the fortress wall, but fortunately an officer called Bouchard or Boussard – the records are not precise on this point – was present, and he understood enough about archaeology to recognise that it was an object of rare value. The stone was a flat slab of black basalt measuring roughly 114 × 71 cms, divided into three horizontal registers each of which contained an inscription in a different script. The words were written in two languages (Greek and Egyptian) and three scripts, the Egyptian text being repeated in hieroglyphic and the cursive writing known as demotic. Its importance was thus obvious – it could provide the long-awaited key to the hieroglyphs. The stone was transported to Alexandria and deposited in the house of General Menou, who had it carefully wrapped in cotton and a double thickness of matting.

French academics were wild with curiosity to see the stone, but crossing the embattled Mediterranean was virtually impossible at the time and the best that could be done was to have the stone coated with printing ink and a number of copies made for dispatch to France. Before the original could follow, the French enterprise in Egypt came to an inglorious end and among the capitulation terms imposed by the British victors was the surrender of a selection of antiquities including the Rosetta Stone. The French were dismayed, as well they might be. At first they tried to insist that it was private property and as such, not subject to a government sequestration order, and when this claim was over-ridden they became determined that if they could not have it, no one else should. The packing cases were broken open, the padding stripped off and the stone tumbled out.

The existence of an immeasurably ancient and highly evolved civilisation in Egypt had never been unknown, but it did not become a subject of widespread fashionable interest or intensive scholastic study until the end of the 18th century. Napoleon's military expedition to Egypt included a team of savants led by Vivant Denon (the frontispiece of his subsequent book is shown here) whose publications made dramatic news of Egyptology.

Alarmed at the possible consequences of this manhandling, the British officer in charge of the transfer went into Alexandria with a cart and a detachment of artillery men who are reported to have enjoyed the expedition hugely, and carried the stone off to his own quarters. The vanquished French now decided to accept defeat gracefully, there being little alternative, so the British could afford to be generous when they were asked for permission to take a cast of stone. This was done; the casts and prints were sent to Paris and the Rosetta Stone to London, where it was displayed for a while at the premises of the Society of Antiquaries before it finally came to rest in its present home at the British Museum.

Even with the aid of this inscription repeating its text in a known and an unknown script, a long time passed before success was finally

achieved. Hieroglyphic studies had always been handicapped by lack of understanding of the nature of the signs. No one knew whether each symbol represented a whole word, a syllable or a single letter, and exclusive adherence to any one of these three theories brought a number of investigations to a dead end. Perhaps the most creditable of these first attempts on the stone was that of Thomas Young, a Cambridge physicist with a deep interest in ancient Egypt. Since the demotic panel had suffered less damage than the other two, Young concentrated on this one.

He began by familiarising himself with the contents of the inscription by studying the Greek text. It was nothing very significant from a historical point of view, being a short commemorative piece set up in 197–196 BC by a group of Memphis priests to record the bene-

The Egyptian people's obsession with death and eternity encouraged the early development of the hieroglyphic script, which could be effectively transcribed in the timeless medium of stone. The funerary chapel of Seti I at Karnak is covered with records of the king, in signs carried out in low relief. Groups of signs enclosed in an oval frame known as a cartouche are royal names and titles.

When the British finally obtained permanent possession of the Rosetta Stone, one of the first scholars to make any worthwhile contribution to its decipherment was Thomas Young. He failed to recognise the varied and complex nature of the signs, but took a considerable step in the right direction when he realised that the cartouches enclosed royal names and titles.

factions and honours of Ptolemy V Epiphanes. Once Young knew what the inscription was about, a close study revealed that certain words were repeated; chiefly names such as Ptolemy, Cleopatra, Alexander and Alexandria, and important nouns such as 'king'. The most useful of these repetitions was that of the words Alexander and Alexandria, which occurred close together in the Greek text. He therefore searched the demotic for a group of similar but not identical signs in what he hoped was the appropriate part of the text (it must be remembered that he had to guess whereabouts to look, since no one was even sure whether or not it should read from top to bottom, left to right or vice versa). Once he had located these signs he had a starting point, and from there he was able to continue to identify and translate a number of other words and letters.

His transcription, published in 1814, included several mistakes which arose from his belief that the demotic text was a word-for-word translation of the Greek—it was in fact only a rough paraphrase. However, his achievement was significant, and one of his discoveries was to prove outstandingly useful. Certain words, he noted, were always enclosed in an oval ring which came to be known as a cartouche, and he established that these rings surrounded the names and titles of royalty. This was as far as the English scholar could go, and for the next eight years the problem was largely abandoned as insoluble. Then in 1822 an official of the Académie Royale in Paris received and published a communication headed *Lettre à M. Dacier relative à l'alphabet des hiéroglyphes phonétiques.* It was a clear, perfectly reasoned and absolutely

undisputable piece of scholarship in which the elusive script was finally deciphered, and its author was a young man from Figeac called Jean-François Champollion.

Everything about this extraordinary man's career gives an uncanny impression of his having been destined for this one great achievement. He was only 11 years old and already an advanced student of Latin, Greek and Hebrew when he first came into contact with the hieroglyphs. At the time he was living in Grenoble with his self-effacing brother who had devoted all his own considerable talents to furthering the boy's development. Here he was introduced to a scholar, J.-B. Fourier, formerly a member of Napoleon's Egyptian expedition, who showed him some inscribed fragments of papyrus. Eagerly questioning Fourier, Champollion learned that no one could read the mysterious script and promptly declared that he would do it himself.

From this time onwards he set himself to study ancient history and languages—Chinese, Parsee, Arabic, Coptic, Pahlavi, anything that seemed to offer any clues to the affiliations of the ancient Egyptian language and script—until he was 17. Wishing to apply for a transfer to study in Paris, he was required to present an essay to the faculty of the Grenoble lycée, and met this challenge by producing a plan for a full-length book on pharaonic Egypt. His teachers were so impressed that instead of admitting him as a student they made him a faculty member on the spot and set him on his way to Paris with high hopes, soon to be brilliantly realised.

At this time he spent only two years in Paris, but he managed to crowd them with more activity than most students encompass in a lifetime. He could command neither patronage nor money beyond the meagre supplies his brother could send, and was often cold, hungry, sick, ill-clothed and worse-housed, but nothing deflected him from his ferociously single-minded pursuit of the intellectual equipment he would need for his attack on the hieroglyphs. He was horribly alarmed in 1808 to find that he was liable to be conscripted into Napoleon's army; but the draft board was accessible to reason and were finally persuaded by those who understood his potential that he might serve France in a more useful capacity than that of cannon fodder. An even more severe shock followed shortly, when he was told by a friend that he was too late, since a book had just appeared in which the hieroglyphics were deciphered. It is easy to imagine his frustration and despair as he rushed to buy the fatal volume—and his laughter, half derisive and half relieved—when he read it and found it to be a farrago of nonsense.

When he returned to Grenoble at the age of

19 to take up his appointment as professor of history, he had not yet made a serious attempt on the Rosetta Stone. With impressive self-discipline he managed to hold back from the endeavour to which he had dedicated his whole life until he was sure that he had nothing left to learn that might be useful to him in his task. He was perhaps obliged to wait longer than he could have anticipated, for the political upheavals attending the fall of Napoleon made steady application to scholarship virtually impossible for him for some years. He had never made a secret of his contempt for the Bourbons, and apart from this, Napoleon's personal interest in his work would have been enough to prejudice his standing with the new régime. His colleagues were too jealous of this adolescent prodigy's brilliance to be inclined to protect him, and as a result he was ejected from the university. This enforced Sabbatical gave him the free time he needed, and by now he felt that he was ready. For six years he alternated between intensive study of the Rosetta Stone, academic teaching and periods of political eclipse until in 1821 he completed and dispatched the epoch-making letter to M. Dacier.

Like most truly great discoveries, the key to the problem of the hieroglyphs seems absurdly simple – once a genius has shown the way. Champollion's boldest stroke, and the one which put success within his reach, was totally to discard the only known ancient 'authority' on the hieroglyphs. This was a Greek named Horapollon who wrote a work on ancient Egyptian symbols in the 4th century AD. It seems probable that there were a few Greeks who could read hieroglyphics, especially in the Ptolemaic period when contacts between Egypt and Greece were frequent and a Macedonian sat on the throne of the pharaohs, but if there were, none of them left any record until Horapollon. The Greek root of the word 'hieroglyph' merely means 'sacred carving', but every later scholar took it for granted that the book *Hieroglyphica* referred to Egyptian writing; starting from this basic assumption they saw every sign as representing a complete word as classic Chinese ideograms do, and this misapprehension led them hopelessly wide of the mark. As early as 1815 Champollion realised the truth. Not only was Horapollon's accuracy doubtful; his book was concerned with Egyptian symbolism and iconography, and despite its misleading title, had nothing to do with the ancient script. Disabusing his mind of all preconceived ideas, he approached the problem afresh.

His starting point was the cartouche – the only work by a previous scholar of which he made any use. He selected as a beginning the royal name of Ptolemy (in Greek Ptolemaios) and Cleopatra, which he chose because they had so many letters in common. Having established that hieroglyphs could be written from left to right or from right to left, but were to be read in the direction which the pictorial signs faced, he compared the two names. The first letter of Cleopatra, he deduced, should not occur at all in the Ptolemy cartouche; it did not. The second letter should have corresponded to the fourth of Ptolemy, which it did. The fourth letter of Cleopatra's name should have been the same as the third of Ptolemy's, and this proved to be the case; and so on. The Greek inscription told

'Forty centuries are looking down on you!', Napoleon harangued his troops at the foot of the pyramids just before the start of one of the battles in his ill-omened Egyptian campaign. He had a shrewd, if somewhat cynical eye for effect, and for international prestige, and this, rather than any abiding interest in the subject, caused him to lend countenance to the studies to which his campaign gave impetus.

him roughly what each word should mean, his knowledge of Coptic, which is very close to the language of the Rosetta Stone, gave him the sound value, and from these beginnings he was able to translate the ancient script which had baffled the academic world for so many years.

The student of hieroglyphics is not faced with a simple alphabet. By the time the Rosetta Stone was carved the script already had a life-span which could be counted in millennia rather than centuries, and during this time it had evolved a daunting number of complications. There was a minimum of three ways in which a word could be used. In English-language terms, the word 'man' can be taken as an example. A small picture of a man could stand for the whole word, conveying the meaning by an ideogram. Alternatively the sound divorced from the meaning might form part of another word, e.g. the second half of the word 'human', and here the same sign would be used for its sound value. Lastly the word could be spelled out alphabetically using the letters m, a and n. The Egyptians had found that alphabetic signs were essential when their culture began to widen out and include foreign names and concepts for which there was no Egyptian equivalent, and these signs were the bases of Champollion's triumph.

By the time of the Ptolemies, Egyptian writing included ideograms, syllabic and alpha-betic elements, and many others. It had begun, at a date too early to determine, as the simplest form of picture writing. However, pictures of objects are liable to misconstruction and further-more, there are many concepts which cannot be visually conveyed. Picture-signs came to be used for the sound value of their initial letters, as the Greek 'beta' and the Hebrew 'beth' give the sound b. They could also convey groups of two or three letters, and in addition a number of determinative signs were adopted. For instance, a picture of a scribe's writing materials clearly denoted something to do with writing, but no one could be sure whether it meant the activity, the equipment or the performer until the sign of a man kneeling in the scribe's attitude was added to clarify the meaning. The determinatives could be very specific like the 'scribe' sign, or more general, denoting a class of object or action. Lastly and more rarely they might be phonetic, and these give us our few clues about the pronunciation of ancient Egyptian which, since the script has no vowels except in the alphabetic forms, can usually only be guessed.

Champollion's ideas were too far in advance of his time for immediate universal acceptance. The apparent simplicity of his conclusions led to their contemptuous rejection by a number of scholars who were quite eminent enough to know better, and his early death in 1832 denied him even the satisfaction of seeing the publication of his book on Egyptian grammar, which did not appear until four years later. These disappointments, however, were mitigated by an event which must have provided considerable consolation. In 1829 he led an expedition to Egypt where he had the opportunity of testing his work in the field and finding it amply vindicated. He made no striking new discoveries, but members of his team attested that, faced with the monuments he had studied for so long in the distant seclusion of the universities, he was like a man returning to a long-familiar landscape. He named and dated buildings, un-erringly picking out Old and New Kingdom work from Roman and Ptolemaic. His en-thusiasm never overpowered his discrimination, for he accurately noted the differences between high-quality craftsmanship and inferior late productions. With his dark skin and golden-brown eyes, even his appearance seemed appropriate to the setting, and his colleagues never forgot the experience.

France was more generous with recognition than the rest of the world, and soon after his return a professorship of Egyptology was specially created for him at the Collège de France. His enjoyment of this honour was tragically short, and when he died his decipher-ment was still being widely disputed; but not for

The set mouth and wide eyes, focussed on some distant objective invisible to ordinary men, seem to reflect the character of Jean François Cham-pollion, the brilliant young scholar whose incisive mind, original approach and encyclopaedic learn-ings were devoted to seeking and finding the key to the Egyptian hieroglyphs. Most of his work was done in France, but friends and colleagues testified that when at last he was able to visit the monuments of Egypt, he seemed like an exile coming home.

above For centuries Egypt
was a land of mysterious
fascination. Its remains,
so vast and enigmatic, so
little understood, alter-
nately baffled and en-
chanted scholars and
travellers, who realised
that an immemorial
history lay behind such
monuments as the pyra-
mids and the sphinx. The
hieroglyphs surrounded
them tantalisingly, but
the key was not found
until the early 19th
century.

Napoleon's troops, shown
here with a somewhat
unconvincing colossal
head in an engraving
dated 1798, were not
notably impressed by the
ancient grandeur with
which they were sur-
rounded. While the
scholars assiduously
measured, mapped and
recorded, the artillery
employed brief intervals
in the hostilities to use the
monuments for target
practice.

long. Gradually one scholar after another looked into his work and found, sometimes against their own determined prejudice, that it would withstand any test they could apply to it. The great German Richard Lepsius was perhaps the most distinguished supporter of Champollion's claims. In 1866 another Rosetta Stone, in the form of a decree of Canopus which was also written in hieroglyphic, demotic and Greek, was found, and Lepsius' work on this text confirmed all Champollion's findings beyond doubt. After this, universal acknowledgement could no longer be denied.

Egypt had a consecutive and detailed written history long before any other European or Near Eastern country, and its records are of incalculable value to other disciplines in supplying, among other advantages, the possibility of accurate dating. In Bronze Age Greece, for instance, it can usually be said that one potsherd is earlier or later than another, but an absolute date is difficult to fix. Once in a while, however, an Egyptian object marked with a royal title is found among trade imports acquired by the Greeks and this, by reference to Egypt's written history, pinpoints a date from which many others can be extrapolated. A modern Egyptologist could not easily converse with a New Kingdom scribe because of the pronunciation difficulties described earlier, but they could readily exchange written communications, thanks to Champollion's work. The whole field of Mediterranean archaeology owes an immense debt to the intense young scholar from Figeac who made possible this direct approach to the ancient world.

The delta town of Rosetta would not have been distinguished in the annals of art or history if it had not been the site of one of the world's most epoch-making linguistic discoveries. It was here that, during the hurried repairing of the fortifications, a young French officer noticed a black basalt stone engraved in three registers, each bearing a different script—the Rosetta Stone.

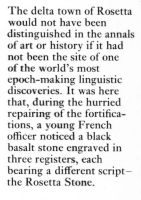

opposite The Rosetta Stone, now in the British Museum, conveys no very significant historical information, but it may well claim to be considered the single most important find in the history of Egyptology. Set up to record the benefactions of Ptolemy V Epiphanes, it paraphrases the same text in hieroglyphics (the formal script of ancient Egypt), demotic (the cursive script) and Greek, which provided a point of departure for the decipherment of the unknown characters.

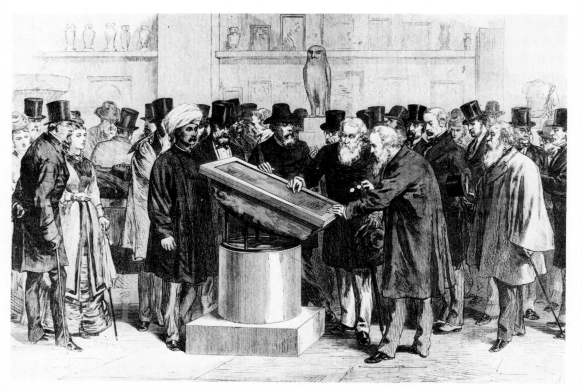

French and English fought over ownership of the Rosetta Stone for some time. In the end, academic honours fell to the French, for though the English gained possession of the original, they were not able to profit by it until Champollion showed the way. From this time onwards the stone has been one of the great attractions of the British Museum.

The jungle cities of the Maya

There is a tendency to describe John Lloyd Stephens, the New York lawyer who put the Central American civilisations back on the archaeological map, as if he had been the first white man ever to gaze on the ruins of a long-lost and forgotten culture. Such descriptions have a fine dramatic ring to them, but they are not true, for from the time of the Spanish conquest onwards knowledge of the native Indians, their predecessors and contemporaries, had never been lost. Stephens' great achievement was in assigning them to their true place in the scale of archaeological, historical and artistic importance.

When the Spaniards arrived in the New World they were confronted (if they had stopped for a moment to think about such considerations) with a unique phenomenon: a Stone Age culture at an immensely high level of social and artistic development with a technology which had remained virtually unchanged for well over a millennium. Received by the Aztec emperor with a stately courtesy not usually accorded to interlopers, they had an unrivalled opportunity for studying the beliefs, language and customs of a people whose civilisation was totally different from anything they had known before. But they did not see the great cities, the massive temples and intricate stone carvings, the brilliant arts, the complex social laws and sophisticated systems of calendrical calculations; they only saw 'savages' who were a rich potential source of gold or converts, and in their rapacious pursuit of both they blindly destroyed, looted and massacred until, within a tragically few years, they had reduced a great empire to a handful of backward and illiterate peasants.

With awesome vitality the jugle flooded over the cities and no one saw any reason to halt its progress. Irreplaceable ancient manuscripts were zealously collected and burnt by missionary priests acting on the profound conviction of their own righteousness in wiping out not only the records of Central American history but even the last vestiges of literacy in the Maya script, so that the few texts which survived the holocaust were effectively silenced.

Everything of value that could be removed had long since been dispatched to Spain, frequently to end up at the bottom of the ocean or in the hold of an English privateer, and soon scarcely a visible trace remained of the greatness which had flourished before the Spaniards' arrival.

Despite all the years of vandalism, however, the existence of the jungle cities was never forgotten. From time to time a friar in search of souls, a trader looking for goods or an explorer seeking for adventure would come across these majestic ruins and now and again a description would be written or a memorial prepared, which hardly anyone troubled to read. In 1558 Fray Antonio de Cuidad Real visited Uxmal and was so impressed that he wrote a lengthy manuscript on its 'very renowned edifices' which he sent home to the Spanish government. The archives swallowed his work as effectively as the jungle had done the edifices in question, and it was not to see the light of day again until 1875. Another priest, Diego Lopez de Cogolludo, made a detailed study of Maya religion and history which he published in 1688, and 100 years later an official team led by the enterprising Capitan Del Rio went to examine the ruins. Reaching Palenque after an appalling journey he set about clearing the site, and made enough inroads on the vegetation to satisfy himself that he had revealed everything worthy of notice. His ingenuous report followed its predecessors into the oblivion of the Spanish archives, apart from a single copy which ultimately fell into the hands of Count Frédéric de Waldeck.

The count appears to have had more than his nobility in common with Baron Munchausen, for his life until the 1820s is a crowded tale of dramatic and totally unsubstantiated incidents. He was, however, unquestionably a widely travelled explorer and an accomplished draughtsman within the limitations of the artistic canon of his day. He followed Del Rio to Palenque and many years later published *Voyage pittoresque et archéologique*, copiously illustrated with his own drawings which proved to be far more *pittoresque* than *archéologique*. By

opposite Trained as he was in the academic schools and classical sites of Europe and the Near East, Frederick Catherwood had the utmost difficulty in getting to grips with the weird and unfamiliar art of the Maya sculptor. Even with the aid of a camera lucida, he had to put in long hours of laborious experiment before he reached a visual understanding of its strange and exotic forms, but once he had mastered the style he produced drawings whose detail and accuracy compare favourably with modern photographs of the Copán stelae.

imposing the severe and intellectual forms of Neo-classicism on Maya art he achieved a bizarre effect which was considerably heightened by his obsession with elephants. Convinced that the Maya culture was closely related to Hindu antecedents and believing that where there are Hindus there must be elephants, he interpreted every form he could not understand (and there were many of them) accordingly.

The survival of the ruins, then, was not and never had been a secret. The only point in question was their significance. To most scholars this was non-existent. They were airily dismissed as the work of savages, and therefore of no conceivable interest or importance. The few who gave any thought to the matter at all were exclusively occupied in trying to fit the culture into some comfortably familiar Biblical or classical framework since they could not believe that any merit existed outside this pattern. Theories, each one crazier than the last, were freely offered, chiefly by people who had never been there or seen the remains they were so judiciously classifying. The Central Americans were Phoenicians, Egyptians, Chinese, Romans or (perhaps the hottest favourite) the Lost Tribes of Israel, the last-named flight of fancy

being based solely on the fact that the Aztecs were known to have Semitic-looking aquiline noses. This was the sort of information available to Stephens when he began to plan his expedition in 1839, for he was the first of all these interested parties to think of going to take an objective and scientific look at the subject of the dispute.

John Lloyd Stephens was not a professional antiquarian. He had not even enjoyed the advantages of a classical education, having read and practised law until ill health sent him to the Mediterranean in pursuit of a change of air and scene. His proceedings thereafter were hardly those of a fragile invalid. With intrepid disregard of inconvenience and danger he roamed through Syria and the Levant, up to Russia and across to Paris via Poland. This journey gave him an insatiable appetite for ancient ruins which was only temporarily assuaged by another even more perilous journey of exploration in Egypt, Arabia and Palestine, after which he set off for home, making what he intended to be a short stay in London on the way. Here his Palestinian adventures naturally drew him to Leicester Square to see the show currently running there: the Panorama of the Ruins of Jerusalem, by Frederick Catherwood, Architect.

Rather less than a first-rate landscape artist but considerably more than an architectural draughtsman, the self-effacing Mr Catherwood had also travelled widely in Egypt and the Near East, recording the antiquities as he went in drawings which, although tinged with the fashionable melancholy of the Romantic movement, had great delicacy and accuracy. During his numerous travels he had assembled the material for his panoramas; each of these was a long strip drawing of a famous city which, displayed round the walls of a suitable exhibition hall, set out the well-known buildings and landmarks in their correct topographical position. By a fortunate coincidence the artist was inclined to try his luck in New York at the time he met Stephens, and before long he moved himself, his family and his panoramas across the Atlantic, thus preserving intact one of archaeology's most productive partnerships.

When he began to take an interest in Central America soon after his return to New York, Stephens had never heard of the Maya. Neither had anyone else, for the culture was considered to be of so little significance that it had not even been accorded the dignity of a name. The records were scanty, but enough to fire his imagination and fill him with profound conviction that wonderful things could be found in the jungles of Guatemala, Honduras and Mexico by anyone with the energy and determination to hunt them out. Stephens was richly endowed with both these qualities; money (the

Count de Waldeck's drawings of Maya sculptures are not very informative about the ancient Central American culture, but they reveal a good deal about the count's preoccupation. Unable to come to terms with the art form, he simply imposed his own ideas on the reliefs. Curiously bland Neoclassical figures, disconcertingly crowned on occasion with an elephant's head, reflect his theory of the Hindu origin of the culture.

other essential commodity for voyages of exploration) was also plentiful as a result of the highly successful book he published on his recent Near Eastern travels, and it did not take him long to persuade Catherwood to accept a contract as official artist to the expedition.

Just as they were about to sail Stephens received an unexpected bonus in the form of a government appointment, the American minister in Central America having recently died. He accordingly added the appropriate papers and a diplomatic uniform to his baggage and on 3 October 1839 the expedition left New York.

The present-day visitor to the Maya sites finds modern hotels, a helpful government tourist department, good roads conducting busloads of travellers to neatly landscaped sites and a wealth of informative literature at his disposal. When Stephens and Catherwood arrived at the port of Isabel they were greeted by an indescribable state of chaos and anarchy extending throughout the scene of their projected journey and adding endless political complications to the natural dangers and difficulties of their route. With much of the country in open revolt and the government largely in the hands of a strong-arm régime of illiterate rebels, surly,

suspicious and armed to the teeth, Stephens' diplomatic status might prove to be an extremely dubious benefit.

Their first goal was the ruins of Copán in Honduras, and at the outset they encountered little difficulty in recruiting the services of a guide who knew the way and who assured them that the route was the main road carrying much of the traffic with the interior of Guatemala. This thriving highway proved to be a miserable mule-track over a thickly overgrown mountain on which their animals floundered through a sea of viscous mud, tripping every few paces over a labyrinth of concealed tree-roots. After a while, however, the country opened up and the going became easier. Their problems were now concerned chiefly with food which was alarmingly scarce and dismally monotonous when available, and the local population who were sometimes not only obstructive but openly hostile. Their American credentials commanded little respect, and in any case few of the officials they encountered could read them.

Despite numerous colourful adventures they came at length to the banks of the Rio Copán and saw facing them an immense wall, perhaps 30 metres high, of meticulously worked

Frederick Catherwood, official artist to both of Stephens's expeditions to Central America, made a series of drawings which vividly evoke the conditions of ruined and overgrown sites. Energetic preliminary work cleared some of the vegetation so that at least the outlines of the main structures were visible, but the *teocalli* of the Temple of the Sun (centre) was still covered in rapidly sprouting greenery when this drawing was made.

and set stones. They had reached the out-skirts of the great Maya city of Copán. The buildings they had found were part of the religious complex which formed the heart of every Maya town. Here lived the priestly hier-archy whose pronouncements regulated every aspect of communal life, supported by an agricultural peasantry working the outlying fields. First settled about AD 430, the city flourished for some 400 years. Then the in-habitants gathered up their possessions and abandoned not just this great and thriving city but the whole region, making a long and arduous cross-country trek to start again in the peninsula of Yucatán. No one can be certain of the reason for this extraordinary exodus; the only feasible explanation seems to be that the Maya's primitive farming methods rapidly exhausted the fields on which their lives depended, and they were forced by the threat of starvation to migrate in search of virgin lands.

Standing among the overgrown ruins of Copán, Stephens and Catherwood could know nothing of this complex historical background, but it was overwhelmingly obvious to them at first glance that their faith in the importance of Central American culture was fully vindicated. Jolted for once out of the flowery verbosity of the 19th-century prose style, Stephens blurted out, 'America, say the historians, was peopled by savages, but savages never carved these stones.' They had achieved their aim; but this was not the end–only the beginning. A new civilisation had been discovered, and their duty was to explore, describe and record it.

Realising that they could not tackle this awe-inspiring task without local help and co-operation, they returned to the contemporary 'town' of Copán–six wretched little hovels–and sought out the leading citizen. This was Don Gregorio, a man of acquisitive nature and de-cidedly hostile aspect. He was not at all inclined to be helpful, but was prevailed upon at length to produce the legal owner of the site, who soon realised that the heaps of intractable stones en-cumbering his land might be turned to some advantage. The visiting Americans, he learned, actually wanted to buy ancient Copán, but he was not sure that he dared sell it, for Don Gregorio was whispering dire warnings of the possible penalties attending any dealings with these undesirable aliens. While the owner vacillated, Stephens' plans hung in the balance, so he produced and played his trump card: his diplomatic credentials and his muddy and bedraggled blue uniform coat with its array of gilt buttons. The owner resisted the passport, but the buttons were too much for him and he gave way. Stephens became the owner of Copán in consideration of the sum of $50.

Possession thus secured, the new landlord

enthusiastically set about the investigation of the site, and in a remarkably short time he and Catherwood carried out a survey and produced a serviceable map. Copán, they discovered, consisted of three adjoining complexes of religious buildings, dominated by the stepped pyramid known as the *teocalli* on which the Central American peoples built many of their temples. Around the pyramids were grouped a number of buildings, great stepped courts clearly designed to seat the spectators of some ritual and open squares set about with the extraordinary monoliths, sometimes as much as four metres high, which the natives called idols and Stephens named *stelae* after the carved tomb markers he had seen in Greece.

Anything further from the grave and lucid rationality of classical Greek art would be hard to imagine, and when Catherwood first attempted to draw them he found his long-practised skill had deserted him. All day he stood deep in the mud, trying to find some mental and visual points of reference to enable him to transfer this weird and luxuriant art on to paper. The problem did not lie in the carvings themselves; they were neither crudely cut nor indistinct, but as crisply detailed as the day they left the hand of a true master sculptor many centuries earlier. But the spirit of the work and the motifs which

expressed it were so totally alien that he spent many hours of laborious experiment before he could come to terms with it. In the end, however, he arrived at a rare understanding of the style, and never experienced any difficulties again. His sensitive studies of the Maya sites are so accurate that they are at least comparable with contemporary work.

Among the motifs which baffled Catherwood in his first attempts were a number of strange glyphs. The arrangement of these symbols and the frequency with which they were repeated soon gave Stephens the clue to their function. They were the 'alphabet' of the Central American script. His excitement was intense. Here, perhaps, were the histories of this extraordinary people, whose achievements had been belittled or ignored by so many successive Europeans. He was sure that when the glyphs were deciphered there would be some amazing revelations. As in so many of his surmises, he was right, but he never lived to see his belief vindicated, for the script was not transliterated in his lifetime, nor for several generations – it is not yet fully understood.

Scholars soon realised that many of the glyphs were concerned with the calculation and recording of time. As the facts emerged it became clear that this was the Maya's dominant

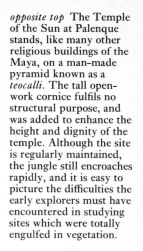

opposite top The Temple of the Sun at Palenque stands, like many other religious buildings of the Maya, on a man-made pyramid known as a *teocalli*. The tall open-work cornice fulfils no structural purpose, and was added to enhance the height and dignity of the temple. Although the site is regularly maintained, the jungle still encroaches rapidly, and it is easy to picture the difficulties the early explorers must have encountered in studying sites which were totally engulfed in vegetation.

opposite bottom A Central American *teocalli* is usually solid, an artificial platform on which great religious ceremonies were performed; but that of the Temple of the Inscriptions at Palenque was a rare exception. Recent investigations revealed a hidden stairway leading down into the heart of the mound to a burial chamber. Inside it lay a sarcophagus, the lid a masterpiece of low-relief carving, containing the magnificently equipped body of an unusually tall man who must, judging by his last resting place, have been a great leader of the people.

The palace at Palenque, where Stephens, Catherwood and their party tried to set up their camp, was once a magnificent complex of corridors, halls and courts with a rare multi-storey tower (reconstructed in recent years), the whole originally stuccoed and painted throughout. The expedition, however, found it far from weatherproof, and so infested with vermin that they were obliged to abandon it in favour of less imposing but more habitable quarters.

One of the unique features of Central American architecture is that its structural elements never make use of any forms derived from plant life, such as the papyrus columns of Egypt or the acanthus capitals of Rome. The so-called Temple of Venus at Uxmal is lavishly decorated with carved panels and columns worked with great mastery of the medium, the motifs being geometric, animal or in the shape of the elaborate glyphs which formed the Maya script.

Even sport had a religious function among the Maya. In the religious complex at Copán was an oblong court walled in on the two long sides. In the centre of each side wall was a stone ring, and the object of the game, played by two opposing teams, was to knock a solid rubber ball through the ring without using the hands. 'Goals' were seldom scored, and when they were, offerings of the losing team's valuables were made.

preoccupation, and that they had evolved the most accurate and complex system the world had ever known. If they had produced nothing else, their achievements in this science alone would have been enough to mark them as a highly developed and sophisticated people, for it made the calendar of the western hemisphere seem positively primitive by comparison. Not for the Maya the clumsy make-weight of leap years to allow for the extra hours and minutes which accumulate annually; they were capable of calculating time-cycles extending for millions of days to within a few seconds.

Stephens was never to learn the secrets of the Maya script, but two weeks at Copán were enough to reveal the general importance of this culture and to whet his appetite for further discoveries. Leaving Catherwood to complete his drawings, he set out for Guatemala city to carry out his diplomatic mission and make preparations for another journey, to investigate the ruins of Palenque in Mexico.

His official duties were simple and soon completed. He merely had to close up the American legation and dispatch all its papers back to New York. Getting the necessary passports and safe-conducts from the ferocious Rafael Carrera, *de facto* President of the Guatemalan republic, was a more alarming process, but by April 1840 it was safely accomplished. The presidential pass was reinforced by letters of introduction from the Archbishop to many of the priests they were likely to meet on the way, and thus fortified on both the sacred and profane fronts, they duly set out.

The road to Palenque was at least as colourful and very much longer than the journey to Copán. It took them nearly a month to reach the settlement, and there was little to justify their expectations when they finally arrived at this dreary jungle village. They were undaunted by the lack of enthusiasm with which they were greeted – they had seen it before at Copán – and only sorry that none of the women could be persuaded to cook for them, for food in that area meant one thing only: tortillas. And making tortillas was strictly women's work. Always prepared to improvise, they stocked up with

The gigantic staircase of the Temple of the Magician at Uxmal (see p. 66) is composed of 100 steps, each 30 centimetres in height but only five in width.

any provisions that could be prepared without female assistance and made for the ruins.

After three hours of struggling along overgrown paths an increasing concentration of carved stones warned them that they were approaching the city. Set on a projecting spur of mountain overlooking the coastal plain, Palenque was, if possible, even more spectacular than Copán. The first building they encountered was the 'palace'. Even at first glance it was clear that they were dealing with architecture of the same culture but a later date than that of Copán. The huge relief carvings on the walls displayed a restraint and refinement of treatment which was absent from the crowded art of the earlier city; they presented no problems to Catherwood who settled down to draw with his usual dedication.

The village was too far from the site for them to commute daily, so they established the expedition's living quarters in the palace. Conditions were less splendid than this dignified address might indicate, for the age-old roof leaked like a sieve, and they had arrived during a season of cold nights and frequent heavy thunderstorms. The prevailing smell of decay and the presence of a number of huge bats in the ruins did not add to their comforts, but worst of all were the predatory insects, from mosquitoes to a particularly virulent mite that burrowed under the toe-nails and into the feet until the victim was entirely crippled. Stephens was so badly afflicted that he had to retire to the village, where he poulticed his swollen feet under the friendly supervision of three sociable and kindly visiting priests. His Protestant soul was shocked by their persistent card-playing, especially on Sundays, but as his acquaintance with them progressed he reached the conclusion that piety, goodness, benevolence and humanity were, perhaps, virtues just as active as strict Sabbath-day observance.

In a short time Stephens was well enough to return to the rain, the mosquitoes and the ruins, and to remain there for nearly a month of intensive investigation and recording. The jungle was so thick that even the enormous stone and stucco mountain of a *teocalli* was invisible until they were able to hack their way almost to the top, but they succeeded in locating several magnificent structures. On top of one pyramid stood the Temple of the Sun, which housed the most remarkable carvings they had yet seen. Here, too, they found another example of the high open-work cornice with which the Maya topped many of their important buildings. In another temple they came across what appeared to be a cross, a discovery which inevitably sparked off a fresh outburst of theorising on the part of the advocates of universal Christianity. In fact, it was not a cross but a stylised tree and the bird associated with it was a *quetzal*, the sacred bird whose fantastically coloured feathers formed the ceremonial capes of the Aztec emperors.

One thing became abundantly clear as they penetrated farther into the undergrowth covering the site, clearing an amazing series of structures and carvings: the resemblance to Copán was no accident. Palenque was well over 300 miles away from Copán, but there could be no doubt that both cities were products of the same culture even though it had reached a more sophisticated and developed form in the Mexican city. The glyphs alone, which were as ubiquitous at Palenque as they had been at Copán proved this beyond question, and the art and architecture confirmed it.

Stephens and Catherwood were not the type to be easily deterred from their pursuit of knowledge, but after a month they were obliged to give up. The rain was now pouring incessantly and the ruins of the palace provided only token shelter, so that sleep was often impossible. Perpetually exhausted, soaked and tormented by mosquitoes, Catherwood became easy prey to malaria and collapsed. They had no choice but to pack up and return to the village where they could at least find the comforts of dry clothes and weather-proof lodging.

Here Stephens tried to emulate his *coup* in buying the site of Copán. His earlier purchase had proved disappointing. He had hoped to detach the carvings and take them down-river to the coast for shipment to New York, but the

One of the rare attractive figures in the crowded and generally gruesome Maya pantheon is the maize god. He is often depicted as a boyish figure, the youthful features carved with great sensitivity and pervaded by a poetic charm unknown among his bloodthirsty fellow deities. He is shown with the curious backward-sloping forehead so admired by the Maya that they used to strap their children's heads between boards to force them into this shape, and the aquiline nose which gave rise to many bizarre suggestions about the racial origins of the Maya in the early days of Central American studies. Dumbarton Oaks, Washington.

opposite A Mayan ball player, probably performing a ritual in honour of the sun god before the beginning of the game. The god of death can be seen in the lower right-hand corner – as time went on, Maya religion became increasingly obsessed with suffering and death. The stakes in the ball game had originally been the clothes and jewellery of the losers, but ultimately they had to sacrifice their lives when a goal was scored by the opposing team. The players were prepared for the game with elaborate applications of protective pads and bandages on ribs, knees and other joints for the ball, which might be as much as 20 centimetres in diameter and could inflict considerable damage. Museum für Volkerkunde, Berlin.

The so-called Temple of the Magician at Uxmal gets
its name from the local people, who told the early
explorer de Waldeck that it was called the Tower of the
Magician. The colossal staircase provided a precipitous
ascent to the sacrificial temple that once stood on top,
dominating the city's religious complex.

Quetzalcoatl, the plumed serpent, the great god and founding father to the Toltec people, was called Kukulcan by the Maya who followed them. Here, at Chichén Itzá the snake appears in its most ferocious aspect on either side of a stairway, its head projecting from the bastions as if to defend the approach.

Rio Copán was fast-flowing and full of rapids, and the scheme had to be abandoned. There was no river at Palenque, but transport prospects seemed better, and he began to make enquiries. Mexican law, he learned, prohibited the sale of land to aliens unless they were married to a Mexican wife. A less dedicated archaeologist might have found this obstacle insuperable, but Stephens, nothing if not enterprising, promptly began to inspect the local talent. He did not record why his pursuit came to nothing. Perhaps his companions dissuaded him; but after a short time he abandoned his matrimonial plans and decided it was time to turn his back on Central America and make his discoveries known to the world.

They reached New York at the end of July 1840 and by May 1841 *Incidents of Travel in Central America*, text by J. L. Stephens and illustrations by F. Catherwood, was ready for the publisher. It was a lengthy book but it had been written in such haste that it had a freshness

restless curiosity had their effect on Stephens. He contacted Catherwood and together they planned a new expedition, this time to the peninsula of Yucatán.

Their starting point was the site of Uxmal where they camped out as before in the ruins of the palace. For six weeks they pursued their researches, uncovering and exploring a series of magnificent ceremonial buildings and courts which displayed a close cultural affinity with the remains they had studied on their first journey. Now they enjoyed two major advantages which they had previously lacked: Cogolludo's *Historia de Yucatán* which recorded valuable details of the area at the time of the Spanish conquest, and a local woman to cook tortillas for them. These notable comforts, however, were no protection against a familiar enemy, and one by one the explorers collapsed and were carried away suffering from malaria, until only Catherwood and the cook were left, one phlegmatically plying his pencil while the other shaped tortillas. Finally he too succumbed and Uxmal was abandoned once more to the victorious mosquitoes.

They did not have to go far in search of other ancient sites, for the whole area had once been thickly inhabited, and they were directed from one ruined town to another, discovering fresh marvels wherever they went. Among the most spectacular of their finds was the *cenote*, or well of Bolonchen. Yucatán has little or no surface water, but here and there a deep shaft from ground level runs down to the water table where supplies can always be found, and the ancient and modern settlements were always established close to these wells. The shaft at Bolonchen was a particularly striking example. A clear 70 metres deep and some 20 metres in diameter, it was spanned from top to bottom by a tremendous wooden ladder, wide enough for 20 men abreast on each rung, up which ceaseless relays of the local people climbed with their water pots on their heads.

Beguiling though these discoveries were, they were not the chief aim of the voyage to Yucatán. What Stephens really wanted was to examine the site of Chichén Itzá. The published records were few, but they all mentioned this city with awe as the greatest and most remarkable in the land, and he was determined not to go away without exploring it. Their most outstanding discovery was also one of their easiest, for the site lay barely 96 kilometres from the sea and the surrounding plain produced a comparatively low scrubby vegetation as opposed to the riotous jungle growth of the interior. There was even a road of sorts from the town of Valladolid to Chichén Itzá, so that in a short time and with relatively little difficulty they found themselves surveying the whole breath-

and spontaneity which was rare among instructive volumes of that time. Stephens' unaffected wonderment at the works of the Maya shone through every line, and his enthusiasm was so infectious that the book became a runaway success on both sides of the Atlantic. The fog of obfuscating theories which had obscured the subject for so long rapidly dispersed, and he found himself almost overnight the leading authority on Central American archaeology. A few months later, public demand and his own

pages 70–71 The *teocalli* at Chichén Itzá dedicated to the plumed serpent Kukulcan (see p. 67) is seen here from the platform of the Temple of the Warriors, where the god Chac Mool reclines guarded by serpents.

Vividly expressive of the savage inhumanity of later Maya religion, the figure of the rain-god Chac Mool reclines with an offering tray in his lap, his face with its unwavering stare and coldly inscrutable expression turned watchfully forward. This carving so impressed the contemporary sculptor Henry Moore that for some time his work showed its influence. Museo Nacional de Antropología, Mexico City.

taking site from the top of one of its buildings.

For several square kilometres in every direction gleaming stone buildings rose above the scrub while innumerable mounds indicated the presence of others. On the whole they showed the same characteristics as the other Maya towns, but there were elements here which Stephens and Catherwood had never seen before although their experience was by now considerable. There was the Caracole, a round tower of unique architectural form with its internal spiral stair, now believed to be an astronomical observatory. There was the so-called 'Nunnery', a massive three-storey building full of small separate cell-like rooms, and the huge temple-pyramid of the god Kukulcan, from which a road, overgrown but still clearly definable, ran to the brink of the vast, sinister, sacred *cenote*.

Beyond these Stephens found a curious oblong court measuring about 90 by 60 metres. It was bounded on both the long sides by a tall wall, high up in the middle of which was a massive ring of carved stone. He had seen something of the kind before at Uxmal, but it was only at Chichén Itzá that its purpose struck him. He found himself reminded of some form of gymnasium or tennis court, and later on his surmise was confirmed by one of the Spanish chroniclers, who described a game played throughout Central America with great pomp and ceremony. The object was to knock a rubber ball through the hole in the stone ring using only the hips or elbows. Needless to say, this was seldom achieved, which is perhaps as well since the defeated team had to pay dearly whenever a 'goal' was scored. At first they were only required to hand over their robes and jewels, and the reliefs suggested a good deal of high-spirited horse-play as the victors claimed their spoils. As time went on, however, and religion became increasingly obsessed with blood, suffering and death, it became the custom to offer the losers as a human sacrifice in the temple adjoining the ball court. Few sportsmen can have played in such deadly earnest, or with more will to win than the ball-players of Chichén Itzá.

When the Maya people abandoned their earlier homes and migrated to the Yucatán peninsula they adopted the city of Chichén Itzá as one of their chief centres. The religious complex here can be viewed from the top of the Castillo, which looks down on to the Temple of the Warriors. This unusual structure is surrounded by hundreds of columns, and rises in several terraces to the shrine at the top.

The loss of most of the written records of the Central American cultures has led to the adoption of some curious names, arbitrarily and often quite inappropriately imposed on buildings of unknown function because of a fancied resemblance to some European counterpart. Several of the sites have a so-called 'nunnery', such as this one at Chichén Itzá, thus named because the design consists predominantly of long corridors with what appear to be small individual cell-like rooms opening off them.

Perhaps the most extraordinary structure on the whole site was the one which is now known as the Temple of the Warriors. As Stephens was wandering through the undergrowth he came upon a two-metre-high stone figure of an armed man, then another and another until he had counted nearly 400. These grim guardians had once formed the supports of a covered colonnade leading to yet another temple with carved and painted terraces supported by gaping stone rattlesnakes holding the upper storeys on their raised tails. In front of the uppermost shrine reclined the terrible figure of Chac Mool turning his chilling blind stare out over the city as he awaited the offerings which were laid in the tray on his lap by priests soliciting rain.

They could have spent a life-time (as other explorers did) examining the site, but other considerations called them away, and by mid 1841 they were back in New York and at work on the book which was to make Yucatán a focus of public and academic interest from then on.

As pioneers their work could hardly have been improved. They located, recorded, described and interpreted the evidence of a hitherto overlooked civilisation with an accuracy which smoothed the way for every later worker in the same field, and established its significance beyond a shadow of doubt. Considering that they were tackling completely new material it is surprising how few aspects they left untouched. One of the rare factors to escape their notice was the secret of the great sacred *cenote* of Chichén Itzá. That was left for a later and equally remarkable American explorer.

page 74 Among the most impressive works of classic Maya art are the great stone stelae of Copan. Often carved from a single monolithic block of stone several metres high, they represent a human figure in relief on the front. The back and sides are carved with such luxuriant detail of glyphs and stylised symbols that the uninitiated eye frequently finds the face of the figure the only easily recognisable feature. These stelae are time markers in the elaborate Maya system of calendrical calculation.

page 75 At Chichén Itzá the rain god is set between two gigantic snakes with upturned tails on the terrace of the Temple of the Warriors. In Central American cultures, rain was a matter of life and death, and this god could only be propitiated by the sacrifice of young and beautiful maidens.

Chichén Itzá: treasures from the sacred well

Every generation has its tales of hidden treasure, and every generation has its knowing and sophisticated characters who raise a sceptical eyebrow at mentions of the gold of the Inca, the Templars, the Spanish Main or whatever the current Eldorado may be. While it is true that there have been all too many tragically deluded souls who have wasted their time, money, health, happiness and sometimes even their lives in obsessive pursuit of a golden chimaera, once in a while there occurs a man whose dreams are based on sound and scholarly information, and who seeks the more valuable and durable treasure of knowledge–but stumbles across gold more or less incidentally during the course of his search. One of these men was Schliemann, who set out to find Troy and discovered the so-called Treasure of Priam; another was Howard Carter whose search for the boy king Tutankhamun uncovered the dazzling tomb hoard of the young pharaoh. Still another was Edward Herbert Thompson, who sought and found the truth of an ancient chronicle 18 metres below the surface of a muddy well in a deserted city of Yucatán.

Born in Worcester, Massachusetts in 1856, Thompson was given a technical education and had to acquire all his considerable knowledge of early Central America by his own initiative. Since John Lloyd Stephens' memorable journey to the peninsula and the subsequent publication of his *Incidents of Travel in Yucatán*, interest in the area had revived and several ancient manuscripts had been rediscovered. Undoubtedly the most important of these was the work of the book-burning zealot Fray Diego de Landa. In the 15 years following the Spanish conquest of Yucatán this tireless priest travelled the peninsula preaching Christianity and trying to stamp out all vestiges of the native religion. He gathered together all the illuminated manuscripts and codices in which generations of the Maya had recorded their customs and history, and burnt them in a ceremonial bonfire. The knowledge that must have been lost to posterity in Fray Diego's fires is incalculable, but he made some amends before he died in writing down

his own recollections of the language and practices of the people of Yucatán as he had found them on his arrival. For centuries his text lay neglected in the Royal Library of Madrid until another enquiring priest disturbed its repose in 1863.

Charles Etienne Brasseur de Bourbourg had also been in the ministry in Mexico and Guatemala, but his interest in the country's past was notably less destructive than that of his energetic predecessor. Determined to explore all the available information on the subject, he immersed himself in the Madrid archives and there he found Diego de Landa's manuscript. Brasseur de Bourbourg recognised its importance immediately, and a short time later it was prepared for publication and made available to everyone with an interest in the Maya, which category definitely included the young Edward Thompson.

Among the practices described by Diego de Landa was the one which most angered and disgusted the cleric, the one which is to this day the most repellent aspect of Central American culture, and the only one which provides even the faintest shadow of an excuse for the brutality of the Spaniards' attack on their new subjects: this was the practice of human sacrifice. In the direct terms of primitive thought the belief had arisen that the gift which is most acceptable (and therefore most propitiating) to an angry divinity is that which costs the highest price to the giver, and no material price can be so high as the donor's own blood, pain and ultimate death. From minor but distressing self-mutilations such as tearing the tongue or ear with thorns, the Maya gradually proceeded to increasingly savage acts as their obsession with the imminence of celestial wrath grew stronger. Nothing but human life would appease the gods, and victims were rounded up and dragged to the top of the *teocalli* where their chests were hacked open and the still-beating hearts were torn out for presentation at the altar. The number of offerings and the complexity of the sacrificial ritual multiplied until by the time of the conquest the Maya were ceaselessly engaged

opposite The passion of sacrifice was a strong element in the Maya religious system. Because they believed that nothing pleased the gods more that that which cost the giver most dearly, they would tear their own tongues with thorns set in a piece of twine to draw blood. In this carving a richly dressed priest crouches at the feet of a divinity with the stalk of maize which is to be the reward for these painful devotions.

One-time owner of the site of Chichén Itzá, Edward Herbert Thompson devoted years of his life to the dangerous, exhilarating and wonderfully rewarding investigation of the enormous sacred *cenote* into which victims and treasures were thrown in unimaginable quantities to propitiate the rain god. Peabody Museum, Harvard University.

From the top of the Temple of Kukulcan at Chichén Itzá the sacred way can be seen leading straight to the brink of the great *cenote*. In this vast natural well, so the people believed, lived the rain god, who had to be propitiated with sacrifices of all they held most dear whenever the life-giving rains failed.

in minor wars for no other purpose than that of securing prisoners for these ghastly rites, during which many thousands might be immolated at a single ceremony.

This hideous destruction of captive warriors was not enough for the gods of Chichén Itzá. Close to the city, and linked by a processional way to the Temple of Kukulcan was the sacred

cenote, a huge natural well of roughly oval shape, some 76 by 52 metres in diameter. The rocky sides fell sheer to the surface of the water some 21 metres below, and in the depths of the turbid well lived Yum Chac, the rain god. He demanded more delicate company than the mutilated corpses of prisoners of war, and it was the custom of the citizens, in times of drought, to choose a bride for him from the most beautiful and flawless maidens of the city. The people told de Landa that it was regarded as a supreme honour to be selected for this role, and described the details of the wedding ceremony.

The bride was dressed and adorned in the Temple of Kukulcan, and then taken in procession to the *cenote*, accompanied by music and singing and with a great train of priests, nobles and warriors. On the brink of the well stood a small temple and a platform which slightly overhung the edge, and here the last rites were performed. As the ceremony rose to a crescendo the girl in all her finery was hurled bodily out into the air above the well, finally to plummet into the rain god's embrace. There were some who came back. It was related that those who survived the terrible fall and the impact with the water, and managed to stay afloat for a specific number of hours, were pulled up from the well and were believed thereafter to be in the god's confidence. There can have been few of them.

These facts were well known to Edward Thompson before he went to Yucatán. For years he had devoted all his leisure time to the study of Central American antiquities and his contributions to learned journals finally attracted the attention of the American Antiquarian Society, who recommended him for a diplomatic post which would enable him to make a full investigation of Chichén Itzá. In 1885 he took up his appointment as consul at Merida and entered on more than 30 years of field studies and research. Thompson was not one of the intrepid school of 19th-century explorers who always dressed for dinner and were careful to retain a tiresome awareness of the white man's heritage, no matter how inappropriate the circumstances might be. He adopted the native language and customs with a sincerity and simplicity which attracted the unfailing goodwill and cordiality of the people wherever he went. He became the repository of many secrets which had never before been revealed to an outsider, was initiated into several local mysteries and was able to move freely in areas which the dangerous hostility of the inhabitants had previously made inaccessible.

His casts and photographs of the Maya antiquities attracted a good deal of notice when they were displayed at the Chicago Exhibition of 1893, and among the interested observers was a mid-western meat tycoon by the name of Armour. His support of Thompson's enterprise took the substantial form of a grant which enabled him to buy a vast plantation including the site of Chichén Itzá. As owner of the city which had been the object of his researches for so long, he could now let his curiosity and his imagination range freely. In addition to his practical investigations he spent many hours sitting on the temple steps or wandering in the ruined courts conjuring up vivid scenes of the past, and time and again he found himself drawn along the sacred way to the brink of the great *cenote*. He knew the story of Yum Chac's wedding from the legends and the ancient chronicles, and as he stared down at the enigmatic surface so far below he gradually became convinced that the well could be made to yield wonderful secrets. If the brides of the rain god and so many other precious offerings had been flung into the water, evidence of the rite must still be lying in its depths and with skill, daring and the right equipment, it could be recovered.

Not the man to do things by halves, Thompson set off for Boston. Here he secured the components for a dredge which he planned to erect on the edge of the well to scoop out the mud from the bottom. He realised, however, that the clumsy jaws of the dredge would miss a lot of the smaller objects, and in any case there would probably be irregularities in the bottom of the well which would be inaccessible to a mechanical excavator. To deal with these there would be no substitute for the human touch, and he accordingly set to work to acquire the skills of a deep-sea diver. He was under no illusions about the undertaking; the bottom of the pool must be thick with the mud of countless years accumulation, he would have to work entirely by touch, and any hazards he might meet would be totally invisible and unforeseeable. His sponsors, appalled by the risk, refused to accept any responsibility for the possible outcome, but Thompson was prepared to carry on independently. He wanted trained assistants, and found them in a pair of courageous young Greek sponge-divers from Florida. He also assembled a team of Indian assistants who were hard-working, intelligent and almost as enthusiastic about the project as he was.

There were formidable difficulties to be overcome in moving the equipment to the site and setting it up on the brink of the *cenote*, but at last everything was ready. Thirty pairs of anxious eyes watched the dredge as it swung out over the water which had been undisturbed for so long, and plunged into the mysterious depths. The cranks and chains rattled, the scoop emerged and the boom swung to deposit its streaming contents in the space which Thompson had cleared in preparation. His

Thompson worked on his dredging operations for many weeks before finding any hint of the treasure he sought. His first discovery was a ball of copal resin, the incense which accompanied Maya religious ceremonies. Here a vessel has been filled with balls of copal, each with a bead of precious jade embedded in it. Peabody Museum, Harvard University.

hands trembled as he approached, for he realised, in his own words, that he 'must soon be "that clever chap who recovered the treasures from the Sacred Well in Yucatán" or else the prize idiot of the whole Western Hemisphere'. Meticulously he sorted through the oozing mud from the dredge, and slowly the unwelcome impression grew on him—prize idiot. Time after time the bucket plunged, scooped and rose again, to disgorge nothing but the rotting sludge that nature, not the Maya priesthood, had dropped into the well.

The heap of mud and the stench of decomposition rose, while Thompson's hopes correspondingly fell. Weeks passed, and the scoop still produced nothing but the natural detritus to be found in any stagnant pool, but still the winch clanked and the bucket rose and fell. Then, one wet and dreary day when everyone's spirits were at their lowest ebb, came the first hopeful sign. In shining contrast to the black mud there lay two large balls of creamy copal resin—the incense which was lavishly used by the Maya at all their important ceremonies. Two lumps of copal did not exactly constitute an earth-shaking discovery, but enough to indicate with reasonable certainty that the well had some religious function. Greatly heartened, the workers plied the dredge with fresh vigour and from this time onwards almost every bucketful con-

Metal technology in Central America was rudimentary in the extreme, and any metal find was of major importance. For this reason the large cache of bells, some of copper and some of gold but all ritually 'killed' by the removal of their clappers, was one of Thompson's most spectacular discoveries. Peabody Museum, Harvard University.

tained more incense, some shaped into balls and some in a softer form, still bearing the imprint of the basket containers in which it had been immolated.

Fragments of wooden artifacts then began to appear, and with great jubilation Thompson recognised a Maya spear-thrower. This implement had a handle with a curved hook at the end into which the butt of the spear was placed. When it was whirled in a forward and downward arc the spear was projected forwards with such power that it could be driven clean through the body of a deer. Potsherds, too, were frequently found in the dredge. At first Thompson, with admirable caution, refused to be too excited. They could have been thrown in at a later date by a casual passerby, for plenty of sherds lay about on the surface at Chichén Itzá and he was familiar with the natural urge, particularly strong in small boys, to throw things into ponds. After a while, however, he realised that he was recovering pottery in quantities which far exceeded the possibility of accident or idle ducks-and-drakes players. Some of it must have been fired at a very low temperature for it had dis-

integrated back into its component clay and was only distinguishable as a patch of contrasting colour in the mud. Other pots, however, were recovered intact, and Thompson found a wide variety of types and qualities.

Some had been well made but badly fired, which suggested that the donor did not always go to a lot of trouble or expense with vessels destined for immediate destruction in the well. This impression was confirmed by some of the balls of copal which were found to consist of a thin outer skin of pure resin over a central core of worthless rubbish. More conscientious celebrants had offered vases of superior quality in a thin, fine slate-grey fabric, and a number of intriguing images modelled in both clay and rubber depicting grotesque animals and human figures.

These finds were powerful evidence of religious activity at the *cenote*, but there was still no indication of any truth in the legend of Yum Chac's wedding. Then at last they spotted something white in the mud from the scoop. It was a human skull, and close examination showed it to be that of a teenage girl. Other skeletons followed in ever-increasing quantities, nearly all of them female and touchingly young, although once in a while the heavy-set frame of a warrior was found among the delicate little bones of the rain god's brides. One of the skeletons was entangled with that of an old man, as if the girl had, at the last moment, clung frantically to the priest who was her last contact with this world and dragged him over the edge with her as she fell. Tiny sandals and even shreds of cloth, so heavily impregnated with resin that the water had not damaged them, were also found. In the end they had the remains of more than 90 of these pathetic young creatures, all between 14 and 20 years of age. Thompson was interested to note that the warrior skulls and those of the sacrificed girls were not the same type, which suggested that they were of different origins and perhaps confirmed the belief that alien prisoners of war were frequently captured specifically to provide victims.

Inevitably the time came when the dredge had reached the limit of its potential usefulness. Thompson took soundings which indicated that the bottom of the *cenote* resembled, as he put it, 'a miniature mountain range', and among these hummocks and hollows the steel bucket was useless. There must be plenty of finds still to be recovered, but by now there was only one way to get at them, and he turned to his deep-sea diving gear. The dredge had one last job to do and this was to bring up a few more scoops full of mud and dump them into a flat-bottomed boat which Thompson had designed as a base for diving operations. The barge would hold the results of about 10 plunges of the dredge, and it was then propelled to the side of the well where there was a projection like a tiny beach. After the mud had been searched they turned it out on this area which it gradually extended into a fairly serviceable landing point.

No precautions were neglected; Thompson might be an enthusiast but he was not foolhardy, and every foreseeable stage of the operation was planned and practised in meticulous detail. Notwithstanding all this care, it was a bad moment for the archaeologist when he loosed his hold on the bottom rung of the ladder hanging over the side of the barge and let himself down into the impenetrable blackness which closed about him before he had descended more than a few feet. His mind raced over the possible dangers he might encounter—there seemed to be an appalling number of them—while his hands were busy making the valve adjustments which became necessary as the depth increased. Once he reached the bottom, however, and ascertained that his colleague had arrived safely beside him, he was filled with the joy that comes to a man who knows he is the first to stand in any long-sought and previously inaccessible part of the world. Then came the irresistible surge of curiosity, and he realised that he was now in a position to force the sacred well to surrender its last secrets.

The first objects to attract his attention were a number of large carved stones. He had been aware of their presence even before he dived for they had fouled the dredge several times, and the fact that their smoothness prevented its jaws from gripping them suggested that they were man-made. From his position on the bottom he was able to attach chains by which the stones were hauled up to the surface. When he came to examine them he found that they were indeed fine carvings, one of which, a seated figure, was of such high quality that it reminded him of Rodin.

The next day's haul was on a different scale but equally intriguing. It consisted of a large number of small metal bells, some of copper and others of gold, in such quantities that Thompson reckoned that the bullion alone must be worth several hundred thousand dollars—a consideration which occupied the explorer very little but which ultimately contributed to the dramatic ending of the enterprise. In the meantime he studied his finds with intense curiosity. The Central American people, he knew, were not an advanced metal-working culture; the mining, smelting, forging and casting of ores were peripheral to their technology, this and the absence of the wheel being their main practical disabilities. The rarity of metal work made any surviving specimens all the more important, and Thompson's cache of over 200 metal bells

The burning of incense and the imminence of death were integral parts of Maya belief. Both are reflected in a human skull extracted from the *cenote*. It has been neatly trepanned and used as an incence burner before being offered to the rain god.
Peabody Museum, Harvard University.

Far more precious to the pre-Columbian people than any quantity of the finest gold, jade was treasured as their dearest possession and sacrificed in times of direst need. A carved plaque ritually broken before immolation shows a seated figure with a curiously expressionless face.
Peabody Museum, Harvard University.

was the largest so far known. Most of the bells were of moulded copper, spherical in shape, and had been ritually 'killed' by having the clappers removed before they were thrown into the well. The exact function of the bells he could not ascertain; he believed they might be a medium of exchange—a form of coinage—but

they also recalled the anklets of bells shown on representations of the god of death, which seemed appropriate to their presence in the well.

In addition to the bells he recovered quantities of ornamental gold-work including decorated discs, bowls, diadems, figurines and many other pieces of unspecified use, most of them deliberately buckled or crushed to 'kill' them before they were sacrificed. He remembered a native funeral he had attended at which the dead woman had been dressed in her best clothes, which had then been slashed in several places to 'kill' them in exactly the same way, so that they could accompany her to the next world. Three sacrificial knives from the well particularly impressed the excavators by the fine workmanship of their stone blades and gold handles, but the most exciting of their finds, in their own eyes at least, were the quantities of jade ornaments which came from the lowest levels. How the Maya came by it was a mystery to Thompson, for true jade is not native to the Americas (though nephrite and serpentine are common enough) and there was no doubt that these artifacts were made of the same genuine jade which was so treasured by the Chinese. He thought of a story told by one of Cortez's companions which indicated that the Aztec emperor Montezuma valued a few beads of carved jade far more highly than large heaps of fine gold, and as he looked at the hoard of precious green stone he reflected that a single piece of it was 'worth a thousand times over . . . the hard years spent in solving the mysteries of the great green water-pit whence it came'.

There were seven plaques about the size of playing cards and nine others of the same length but only half as wide, all carved with exquisitely executed figures in low relief, and literally hundreds of personal ornaments: ear, nose and lip plugs as well as beads and pendants. Finest of all was a small figurine in a perfect state of preservation, unlike most of the other jades which had been ritually broken.

Wood and fabric, pottery, jade and above all, the human bones proved that the old stories told the truth about the rain god's home in the sacred well. Besides this, they helped to fill out the picture of life in Chichén Itzá which had hitherto been supplied only by the ruined buildings, and in this respect the small potsherds were just as valuable as the finest jade or massive gold. Unfortunately the government held a different opinion.

Thompson had worked at the site for years before news of incalculable treasure began to filter through to the state officials, but as soon as they realised that they might be missing something good and that a great prize was being spirited away from under their noses, fast and

drastic action followed. Thompson himself was not at Chichén Itzá at the time, which was as well for him, since the government not only impounded the whole of his estate and its contents but seized on his friends and colleagues who were still at work there. He was not the man to be easily intimidated, nor to abandon his friends when they were in trouble. He worked out that he could pick them up and get them away by sea if he could obtain a boat, but all he could find was a flimsy half-finished craft which was, at best, only equipped for the shortest coastal runs. However, the deep blue sea seemed preferable to the governmental devil, and he acquired the boat and set out. He rescued his associates and after a number of hair's-breadth escapes and a terrifying voyage they all arrived safely in Cuba, never to revisit Yucatán and the city of the sacred well.

This was not the end of the matter. The Mexican authorities, infuriated at the thought of the treasures which had been abstracted, launched an angry demand for restitution at the United States in general and the Peabody Museum at Harvard in particular.

For years the case dragged on in the international courts, ending in a decision in America's favour which caused protracted bitterness between the two nations until the USA voluntarily restored a large share of the finds to their home. Thompson, however, as the author of all this mischief, knew he would never be admitted

to Mexico again, and the rest of his life was spent in pursuing his study of Central American civilisation from the materials available in the United States. His years at Chichén Itzá, however, had produced a brilliant contribution to knowledge and ensured him an honoured place in the history of Maya archaeology.

THE BIBLICAL DELUGE AN ASCERTAINED FACT.

AN AUTHORITATIVE SURVEY OF REVOLUTIONARY DISCOVERIES ON THE SITE OF KISH, A CITY FOUNDED NOT LATER THAN 5000 B.C.

By Dr. STEPHEN LANGDON, Professor of Assyriology at Oxford, and Director of the Oxford-Field Museum Expedition to Kish.

(See Illustrations on the opposite page, and Coloured Illustration on page 1.)

THE remarkable results of this expedition last season have already been partially communicated to the public, and in this article I am able, after having studied the detailed reports of the various members of the staff, to place at the disposal of scholars an accurate survey of the only series of stratifications of a city whose history was continuous from the beginning of history right down to the Parthian period. The issue of *The Illustrated London News*, Aug. 31, 1929, pp. 374-5, contained five photographs which showed in promiscuous order some of the discoveries. There were specimens of the fine copper weapons and pottery of the pre-diluvian tombs, before 3300 B.C. A front view of the remarkable but unrestored painted head of a Sumerian (Fig. 2) was also given there. The coloured illustration on page 1 of this number shows this head as restored and its original colouring, drawn by Miss C. L. Legge. I discussed it in the issue of the *Daily Telegraph* for Dec. 13, 1929.

If the reader will consult Fig. 5 (opposite page) he will have before him a view of the left or north side of the deep excavation to water level, sixty feet from mound level, and Fig. 1 shows the right wing of this same excavation. On the inclined ridge left by the excavators to enable the basket-boys to carry the earth from the deep levels to the railway-trucks, which enter at plain level by the cutting seen in the upper left corner (in Fig. 5), stand Mr. C. L. Watelin (left), the head of the staff, and Mr. T. K. Penniman (right), anthropologist. Above the deep trenches the excavations will be seen to have been cut back for the railways to run along the eastern side of the work.

It was in the level along the ridge that the painted head of a Sumerian (Fig. 2), which originally came from below water-level, twenty-five feet lower, was found. From the same level came pictographic inscriptions which we know from my own excavations at Jemdet Nasr, seventeen miles north-east of Kish, to belong to the period of painted pottery found at Kish just below water level. The hair of the head and the full beard are black, the skin a pale reddish-yellow ; the type is armenoid, and so certainly characteristic of the primitive Sumerian sculptures from all other sites that there is no doubt but that it comes from the painted-ware level. Decoration in colours ceased to exist after modern water level, and the evidence proves that the later Sumerians and Semites conserved objects of art and inscriptions from remote periods of their history.

In the *Daily Telegraph* of March 18, 1929, I described and gave a photograph (Fig. 4) of the stratification, 1½ feet thick, consisting of fine river sand mixed with fresh-water shells and rows of small fish, precipitated over the whole area by an inundation. This proved that the whole city some time about 3300 B.C. was covered by a gigantic flood. If the reader will look closely at Fig. 5, right side just below the ridge of plain level, he can see a small portion of this flood layer separating

itself cleanly from the débris of human occupation above and below. It requires a sharp photograph to show this stratum as one sees it in the photograph published by the *Daily Telegraph* (Fig. 4). It runs right across the whole excavation. On top of it lies a red stratum, four feet thick, made of burnt plano-convex bricks. This is, of course, a local stratum and ends with the temple area. It

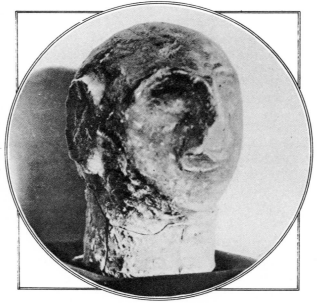

FIG. 1. WHERE EVIDENCE HAS BEEN FOUND CORROBORATING TRADITIONS OF THE FLOOD: THE EXCAVATIONS AT KISH (NEAR THE SITE OF BABLYON), WITH AN ALLUVIAL STRATUM REPRESENTING AN INUNDATION THAT OVERWHELMED THE CITY NOT LATER THAN 3200 B.C.

is the great platform on which the temples and two stage towers were built at Kish after the reconstruction of the city.

FIG. 2. NEW LIGHT ON THE ORIGIN OF CIVILISATION: THE SUMERIAN HEAD (ILLUSTRATED IN COLOUR ON ANOTHER PAGE, BUT HERE SEEN UNRESTORED) — AN EXAMPLE OF PRE-FLOOD PAINTED POTTERY THAT DISAPPEARED AT KISH NOT LATER THAN 4000 B.C.

So many erroneous conclusions have been drawn in European and American journals about early history and chronology based on the excavations at Kish that I communicate in Fig. 3 a plan of the series of stratifications made by Watelin and Penniman. I hope that this will finally make clear the statements previously made in the *Times* and *Daily Telegraph*, and put an end to the absurd deductions about chronology still widely circulated by many scholars. The red stratum is definitely dated by tablets found in it as pre-Sargonic. The deluge stratum is indicated just underneath it, and five metres below this lies modern water level. Fig. 1, in the right lower corner, shows water accumulated there. The excavators sank a shaft eight feet square at this point (as shown in Fig. 3, near right lower corner) nine feet to virgin soil.

Now it is only from the top of this shaft—in other words, twenty-five feet below the pre-Sargonic period of the red stratum (*circa* 2900 B.C.) — that painted ware is found. It is absolutely impossible to date this period after 3000 B.C. Below the flood level to water level, through fifteen feet of débris, there is a continuous civilisation, marked by different types of pottery. Here the skulls are preponderatingly round-headed armenoids, and this ratio increases as they lie deeper. The lower parts of the shaft yield flint implements of the Neolithic age in quantities right down to virgin soil. It is impossible to date the age of any of the painted ware later than 4000 B.C., and the beginning of this city later than 5000 B.C., and perhaps much earlier.

In and above the red stratum the long-headed Semite predominates, but this type is also found below the flood level. Jemdet Nasr, seventeen miles north-east, where painted ware and pictographic tablets were found at modern plain level, of the same period as the Kish stratum below water level, lies in our time twenty-five feet higher than Kish, which was on the old bank of the Euphrates. In ancient times Jemdet Nasr lay not more than twelve miles from the bank of this river. No flood stratum was found there, and the obvious inference is that the great deluge never extended more than twelve miles from the eastern bank of the Euphrates.

Geological survey may prove that this Flood, on which were founded Sumerian, Babylonian, Assyrian, Aramæan, and Hebrew stories, extended over a greater area of the valley below Kish—for example, at Shuruppak, where Xisuthros built his ark and saved his family from the Deluge. However this may be, the Flood destroyed Kish, and certainly all the great cities of Sumer, which were all on the Euphrates. It was a local riverine disaster, but the civilisation above the flood stratum is continuous with that below. There are differences, but these are due partly to the disaster itself, partly to the increasing domination of the Semitic race.

The epic of Gilgamesh

When young George Smith of Chelsea was apprenticed to a firm of engravers in 1854 no one would have foreseen that in his short career he was to become one of the most distinguished Assyriologists of his day. Born in 1840, he had few advantages of education, family influence or money, but Messrs Bradbury and Evans of Bouverie Street, his employers, soon recognised the skill and accuracy of his touch and believed he had a promising future in the business. George, however, did not envisage a lifetime bent over banknote plates; since he was a boy he had spent all his spare time dreaming of Bible lands and studying all the books he could find on the subject. His interest was neither unusual nor surprising except in its intensity, for Assyriology had recently made tremendous advances with the publication of Mr (later Sir) Henry Rawlinson's decipherment of the cuneiform script of Mesopotamia. Before this, large numbers of clay tablets and inscribed stones had been assembled but all attempts to read the script had had only limited success. Rawlinson spotted an immense inscription carved high on a cliff face at Behistun where the early kings of Persia were buried and, making a hair-raising ascent to copy it, found that it was written in three different languages – a western Asiatic Rosetta Stone. His solution to the script soon followed, and the archaeology of the region could then be supplemented by the extensive evidence of the written histories.

Every spare penny of Smith's pay was spent on works on Mesopotamian archaeology from which he could relate the discoveries of the great explorers to the events narrated in the early books of the Old Testament. Books, however, were not enough. Three times a week, when the galleries of the British Museum were open to the public, he would leave Bouverie Street in his lunch hour, hurry across Fleet Street, up Chancery Lane and west along Holborn to the museum to study the original monuments and writings. His attendance was so persistent that after a few years he caught the attention of the Keeper of Oriental Antiquities, Dr S. Birch, who thought such determination should be en-

couraged. He accordingly allowed Smith to work from the sheets of Rawlinson's work *Cuneiform Inscriptions of Western Asia*.

The results of this kindly concession were spectacular. Within a short time – two years at the outside – Smith had mastered both the script and the language. A natural flair of this order, coupled with Smith's dedication and enthusiasm, could not go unrewarded, and he was offered an official post as a 'repairer' in the museum. His employers and some of his friends were appalled. They regarded it as the height of foolhardiness to abandon a secure job in which he could reasonably look forward to financial competence and even a modest degree of fame by virtue of his skill as an engraver in favour of the uncertainties and competitive pressures of the academic life for which he had no formal training. Smith, however, had no such reservations and accepted the offer at once.

The museum owned large numbers of clay tablets, some in good condition, some broken and the pieces misplaced and others again with passages obliterated. Tablets of this kind are extremely fragile. The signs were originally inscribed on clay which was allowed to dry in the sun but not kiln-fired unless the tablet was destined for a place on an important monument, and in consequence the least accident could cause these dried tablets to crumble into dust. Archaeologists found that their purposes were served best by tablets from a building which had been destroyed by fire, because a fierce conflagration sometimes had the effect of a kiln and baked the tablets to brick hardness. It was Smith's new job to organise this mass of fragmentary material, piecing together the broken tablets whenever two edges could be matched and trying to decipher the inscriptions. In time he developed an outstanding instinct for this work based on a remarkably sensitive feeling for the language and culture which often enabled him to grasp the basic significance of even the most battered and illegible texts. Since the museum owned over 120,000 tablets in varying states of disrepair, there was plenty of scope for his talents.

opposite Both the great rivers which enclose Mesopotamia, the Tigris and the Euphrates, are subject to sudden and violent, though usually localised, flash flooding. An event of this nature, built into the folklore of the region, can easily account for the appearance of Deluge stories in the mythology of many different lands, and evidence of flooding has been found at a number of widely separated sites. The flood level found by Woolley at Ur was the wrong date for the Noah story, but that of Kish seems to provide a much likelier candidate.

almost exclusively by Smith. As he worked he made notes of all the inscriptions concerning the Assyrian kings, for he was planning an ambitious project of his own: a history of the 7th-century BC king, Assurbanipal. There was only one obstacle to this scheme, but it was a considerable one. Smith envisaged a volume of cuneiform text with interlinear transliteration and translation, the printing of which would call for a large quantity of cuneiform type. This was prohibitively expensive and the authorities were unwilling to risk such a sum on a young scholar whose name was completely unknown outside the museum. But the problem was solved by the generous support of a banker named Bosanquet and the Egyptologist Samuel Sharpe, who believed in Smith's work so firmly that they agreed to finance its publication.

In the meantime Smith's reputation in the academic world was growing rapidly. He published a number of monographs and read a paper on Babylonian chronology to the newly formed Society of Biblical Archaeology which deeply impressed the members. By 1871 he was forging ahead with the fourth volume of Rawlinson's monumental work when he came across a tablet which, in scholastic importance

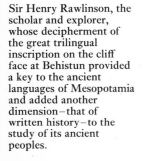

Sir Henry Rawlinson, the scholar and explorer, whose decipherment of the great trilingual inscription on the cliff face at Behistun provided a key to the ancient languages of Mesopotamia and added another dimension – that of written history – to the study of its ancient peoples.

A huge number of scraps of crumbling clay, covered with half-obliterated scratchings of an obscure script that had been obsolete for at least two millennia, would not be most people's idea of enjoyment, but Smith tackled the work with keen enthusiasm and before long was producing order out of this apparent chaos. His working conditions were far from ideal. In his day the tablets, which were later to be mounted in individual numbered boxes with soft linings and glass tops, were kept in drawers where they rattled about and chipped their edges every time they were moved; but the worst of his difficulties lay in finding enough light. The signs were often faint, and curiously enough, in those days of long winter nights and pea-soup fogs, although the rest of London was bright with gas lights, the museum had no artificial lighting at all, apart from a few lanterns reserved exclusively for the use of departmental Keepers. When the dusk closed in everyone was sent home.

Out of these unpromising circumstances there gradually emerged a third volume for Rawlinson's *Cuneiform Inscriptions*. Smith, now promoted to Assistant in the Oriental department, concentrated chiefly on historical inscriptions which had some relevance to biblical studies, and his work helped Rawlinson to produce a volume which attracted such widespread scholarly attention that the museum authorities were encouraged to commission a fourth, the material for which was selected and copied

and general interest, eclipsed everything he had seen before. He was piecing together the story of a character whose name he translated as Izdubar, now identified with the Mesopotamian hero Gilgamesh, a sort of Asiatic Hercules who went about fighting monsters and generally performing epic feats of strength and cunning, when he became progressively certain that what he was reading was nothing less than a Chaldean account of the Deluge, complete with the Ark, the animals, the dove and the raven exactly as it appeared in the Bible. The account was substantially complete apart from a gap of some fifteen lines in the early part of the twelve-tablet series. Birch and Rawlinson confirmed his translation and, equally excited, arranged for the discovery to be announced at the December meeting of the Society of Biblical Archaeology in 1872 which was attended by a highly distinguished audience including Mr Gladstone. The meeting was enthralled, and passed a unanimous resolution urging the British Museum to commission further investigations at Kouyunjik (ancient Nineveh) to look for information with George Smith in charge of the project.

Official bodies move notoriously slowly, and the public was not inclined to await the result of the Museum Trustees' ponderous deliberations. The *Daily Telegraph* decided to act while the news was still hot, and offered 1000 guineas to finance an expedition to search for the missing lines of the Deluge story: an archaeological forlorn hope if ever there was one. Everything was arranged so quickly that little more than a month after the meeting of the Society of Biblical Archaeology at which the whole thing was mooted, Smith left London for the east.

He was a brilliant archaeologist, but as the moving spirit of a scheme like this he had one insuperable drawback–he was a totally, transparently honourable and honest man, and it would have been difficult to imagine anyone less fitted to cope with the corruption and deviousness of the Turkish pashas who controlled Mesopotamia at the time. When he asked for a *firman* (official documentary permission) to excavate and was told, 'You can't have a *firman*,' he believed that this answer meant exactly what it said, while anyone better versed in the ways of the pashas would have known that it meant, 'Make it worth my while and I'll see about a *firman*.' Despite all evidence of its inaccuracy he persisted in this naively

George Smith (1840–76), the banknote engraver who became, in his short career, one of the most distinguished Assyriologists of his day. His work, by linking the Noah story with the Gilgamesh Epic, foreshadows contemporary discoveries connecting the events related in the Old Testament with the legends of other cultures, with whose territories the Israelites had contacts.

Early excavations were carried out with no system and little aim beyond a vague hope of spectacular finds to astonish the public. This engraving of the work in progress on the banks of the Tigris across from the modern city of Mosul probably owes a good deal to the artist's imagination, but as a reflection of the undisciplined and often destructive activity of the first diggers it is, in all likelihood, reasonably accurate.

optimistic view of imperial Turkish official character throughout his time in the east, and thus caused himself endless delay, hardship, annoyance, frustration and even actual danger. His difficulties were complicated by the fact that, although he was happily at home in a number of ancient languages, he spoke little or no Arabic and was therefore seldom able to tackle these problems by direct negotiation.

One is compelled, however, to admire the sang-froid and self-reliance with which this inexperienced and untravelled young man embarked on his solitary journey into the wilder reaches of Western Asia. From the port of Alexandretta he made his way eastwards on horse and sometimes mule-back, contending all the way with inadequate animals, appalling accommodation, bizarre food and recalcitrant guides, underterred by bloodcurdling tales of bandits which were obviously designed to induce him to hire a large party of bodyguards who would probably have been a considerably greater liability than any number of bandits. Sublimely confident that no one would have the temerity to attack an Englishman, he pushed on and, the marauders having predictably failed to

materialise, reached the town of Mosul on 2 March 1873. The mounds of Nineveh lay close by, on the other side of the Tigris.

At Mosul he had his first brush with Turkish officialdom, which was to prove typical of future dealings. Smith had set out with the expectation that a *firman* to excavate was being negotiated by the British authorities and would be awaiting his arrival. Finding that no *firman* was forthcoming, he asked for a guide so that he could go and inspect a neighbouring site, but even in this modest request he met with an obstructive attitude. The pasha adamantly refused permission. Smith must not, he declared, so much as look at the mounds. Finding him 'quite unreasonable about the matter' and with no indication of any action about his *firman* in the immediate future, Smith decided with characteristic energy to make a trip down river to Baghdad where he could promote his own interests in person with the help of the British Resident (there was none at Mosul). This was accomplished in a manner more reminiscent of Huckleberry Finn than the Arabian Nights, on a make-shift raft of wood set over a base of inflated skins and provided with a sort of cabin to

The archaeological sites of Mesopotamia seldom have the immediate romantic or visual appeal of those of the Mediterranean cultures. They were originally built almost exclusively of brick, stone and timber both being in desperately short supply. With the passing of time the bricks disintegrated into dust, or were dug up by the local people for re-use in their own dwellings, so that very little now remains standing in a recognisable form. Nineveh, which lacks even the drama of a ziggurat, suggests little of its former wealth and power.

Layard's investigations at Nineveh made a historical reality of the Assyrians, who had hitherto been just another name in the Old Testament records. He was, however, more concerned with the removal of the palace sculptures than with collecting historical records. Working in conditions of great difficulty he managed to detach and remove several of the immense stone monsters, winged bulls with human heads, which guarded the entrance to the palace of the Assyrian kings.

The collection of carvings and bas–reliefs excavated at Nineveh by Layard and presented by him to the British Museum are a testament to his energy and enthusiasm.

George Smith visited the
site of Babylon during
the innumerable delays
while he waited for the
Turkish officials—usually
venial and always
obstructive—to implement
his documentary permis-
sion to excavate. The site
was a fearful confusion of
tunnels and trenches,
mostly unrecorded, and
several decades were to
pass before an orderly
and fully recorded dig
organised by German
scholars revealed the
details of the ziggurat
(right) and the pre–
Sargonid levels of the
temple area (below).

Early excavations in Western Asia, especially those of Nineveh, produced hundreds of thousands of dried clay tablets inscribed in the recently deciphered cuneiform script. It was Smith's job to sort, transcribe and decipher some of this vast corpus of material, among which he recognised the Gilgamesh Epic, with its unmistakable parallel to the biblical story of Noah's ark and the Deluge.
British Museum, London.

provide shelter, a function which it only marginally performed.

After an adventurous but uncomfortable passage lasting several days he reached Baghdad and the safety of the Residency where the experienced and effective support of Colonel Henry, the Resident, soon produced the results Smith wanted. The matter of his *firman* well in hand, he decided to make the most of his time in the area by visiting the ruins of Babylon, which he found in an indescribably chaotic state, 'furrowed by numerous ravines', and 'traces of chambers, tunnels and passages'. 'No proper efforts', he went on, 'have been made to examine the structure of this ruin, and in climbing through the old trenches and tunnels there is a sense of bewilderment which prevents an accurate survey.' Like all other visitors he marvelled at the vast dimensions of the ancient city and speculated about the probable location of the legendary Hanging Gardens.

Babylon, however, was not the chief object of his visit. When he returned to Baghdad he received the long-awaited *firman* and, after a hurried round of the dealers to buy inscribed tablets, he set off on his way back to Mosul. After all these delays one would have expected him to be only too anxious to attack the mound of Nineveh immediately, but he chose to spend a month or so making exploratory excavations at nearby Nimrud, and it was not until 7 May that he finally embarked on the work for which he had travelled so far.

The site of Nineveh lay on the east bank of the Tigris surrounded on two sides by a curve in the river and the rest by a magnificent circuit wall about 13 kilometres long. Even at this stage in the excavation the palace of Sennacherib, known as the south-west palace, had been identified and the royal library, source of most of the British Museum's tablets, located, and here Smith began his first trenches. Two days later he set another team of workers to investigate the north palace of Assurbanipal. There was little to report in the way of major sculpture or similar spectacular finds (Layard, who first investigated the site in detail, had made off with most of these), but they were not Smith's primary interest. He had come to look for tablets, and there was no shortage of these.

Within a week, while he was rummaging in a pit in the north palace, he came across part of a broken tablet inscribed with a fascinating statement of ancient law, and a little farther along he was fortunate enough to discover the rest of the tablet.

An even more startling revelation awaited him on 14 May, just one week after the opening

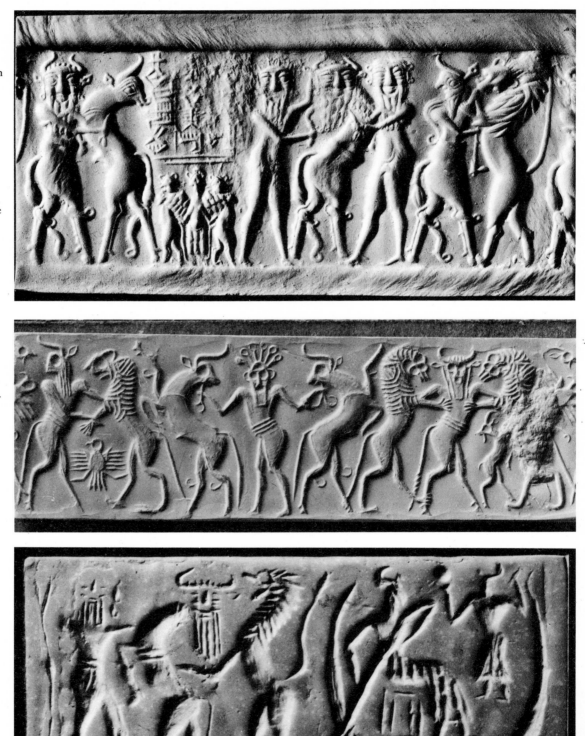

The name of the mythological hero changes according to the culture, but in the art (especially that of seal-stones) and folklore of Sumer, Babylon and Assyria the figure of the hero known to us as Gilgamesh pursues his search for an escape from mortality, the common lot of the human race. During his search he meets an old man (the biblical Noah) who tells him the story of the Deluge and of the ark which was built to survive it. Often overcoming monstrous beasts, sometimes accompanied by his devoted friend, the bull-man Enkidu, Gilgamesh wanders through the legends of Western Asia, only to fail in the end, accepting his fate as a mortal man and recognising that immortality is only for the gods. British Museum, London (middle and bottom); Koninklijk Penning-kabinet, The Hague (top).

of the excavation. As he brushed the dirt from one of that day's haul of tablets from the north palace he realised that it contained material related to the Deluge story, and not only that but precisely the missing lines. Against incalculable odds he had found exactly what he was looking for right at the beginning of his campaign. Triumphantly he telegraphed the *Daily Telegraph* and returned to work, as there was still a great deal to be done. Either the wording of his telegram was altered or the newspaper misunderstood his intentions, but as soon as they received the news they immediately assumed that the mission was now complete and that Smith would pack up and come home, so they withdrew their financial support, while expressing suitably cordial but vague interest in the continuing progress of the work.

Smith was deeply disappointed. For him the Deluge tablet, though a wonderful stroke of luck, was not nearly so important as the new knowledge which might be assembled from the excavation in the future. For instance, in the last few days of the campaign he unearthed a tablet which provided invaluable information about the cuneiform script. It was divided into four columns, the first of which showed the phonetic value of each sign, the second the sign itself, the third its name and meaning and the fourth the ideas or words it represented. This tablet alone, he felt, would have justified the entire expedition. However, with no more funds forthcoming he had no choice but to close the excavation and return to England. On 8 June, hardly a month after he had started his first trench at Nineveh, he took leave of his friends and set off for Europe.

He retraced the long ride from Mosul to Alexandretta and here he faced one of the most unpleasant surprises of his career. The Turkish customs officials looked over his official papers, including the Sultan's *firman*, and promptly confiscated the precious packing cases which contained all his hard-won treasure of tablets. Smith pleaded, reasoned and raged to no avail. The British consul, Mr Franck, was equally powerless to help and in the end Smith was obliged to sail on 19 July, leaving his excavation cut short by its sponsors and all its results in the indifferent hands of the customs officials. It was not until a strongly worded request was made in Istanbul by the British ambassador in person that the packing cases were released, ultimately to arrive safely in the British Museum.

Here Smith was able to examine and collate his new finds, and soon produced his version of the Deluge story. 'Izdubar' (Gilgamesh) is wandering on the coast seeking a cure for the leprosy-like disease with which he is afflicted when he meets a venerable man who relates the tale of the great flood and how he escaped it.

The correspondence between this story and that of Noah in the Bible is unmistakable. The Mesopotamian Noah (Smith translates his name as Hasisadra) tells how a divine presence came to him in the night to warn him of the coming inundation and to instruct him in the making of a great ship to be stocked with all the animals of the world. This Hasisadra did, and at the prophesied time the storm broke. 'The bright earth to a waste was turned ... it destroyed all life from the face of the earth ... the strong deluge over the people, reached to heaven. Brother saw not his brother, it did not spare the people. In heaven the gods feared the tempest and sought refuge.' After seven days the downpour stopped, and Hasisadra continues, 'I perceived the sea making a tossing; and the whole of mankind turned to corruption, like reeds the corpses floated. I opened the window, and the light broke over my face, it passed. I sat down and wept, over my face flowed my tears.' Soon the Ark ran aground on a mountain and Hasisadra began to send out messengers. 'I sent forth a dove and it left. The dove went and turned, and a resting-place it could not enter, and it returned. I sent forth a swallow and it left. The swallow went and turned, and a resting-place it could not enter, and it returned. I sent forth a raven and it left. The raven went and the drying-up of the water it saw, and it did eat, it swam, and wandered away, and did not return. I sent the animals forth to the four winds, I poured a libation, I built an altar on the peak of the mountain ...'

The value of Smith's work was now established beyond question, and since the *firman* did not expire until March 1874 the museum authorities agreed to finance another expedition to make use of its remaining few months. Smith set off again, arriving in Mosul at the beginning of January 1874 with high hopes for further important discoveries. The weather was against him, for it was winter and icy rains often impeded his work seriously, but this was the least of his problems. The local pasha had awakened to the fact that there was a potential source of unlimited graft in this mad Englishman's unaccountable obsession with what he saw as worthless ancient rubbish which lay so thickly around his district, and Smith found himself confronted with an implacable demand that half his finds be handed over to the Turkish authorities and an order to the team of diggers to stop work until these terms were agreed. Smith, reasonable and optimistic as ever, pointed out that half the inscriptions would be useless to either party as complete records were the entire aim of the expedition, and that to confiscate half would ruin the British collection without being of the slightest benefit to the Turks. It never entered his innocent head that

From the earliest Sumerian seals to the art of the late Babylonian empire which flourished between 700 and 500 BC, Gilgamesh continues his restless search for immortality and his struggles with the malevolent beings who are the enemies of his race. A neo-Babylonian terracotta shows the face of one of his adversaries, the demon Humbaba. British Museum, London.

opposite Nearly five metres high, stolid and muscular with the massive strength that befits the warlike civilisation of the Assyrians, a figure of Gilgamesh guards the palace built by Sargon II at Khorsabad in the second half of the 8th century. Under one arm the figure holds a lion, seemingly quite without effort, oblivious of the furious animal's struggles. Musée du Louvre, Paris.

the pasha had not the least interest in owning a heap of crumbling tablets; he merely wanted Smith to buy them back at a suitable price in order to supplement his own meagre and frequently unpaid salary. No wonder Smith achieved nothing by invoking the cause of disinterested scholarship or international goodwill.

Despite all this aggravation he managed at last to get his men out to Kouyunjik and set them to work. He explored several more parts of the palace, discovering pottery, obelisks, broken statues, the remains of a later palace and temple, seals, reliefs and yet more tablets, nearly 3000 of which were unearthed from Sennacherib's library. Official interference continued undiminished, and Smith was now also experiencing considerable difficulties with his workmen who were growing increasingly quarrelsome and obstructive. The *firman* still had another week to run when he gave up the unequal struggle and closed the excavation. Reluctantly handing over a number of tablets to the pasha, who must have been sorely puzzled to know what to do with this unwanted windfall, Smith retraced his steps over the now-familiar route from Mosul to Aleppo, went through the now-familiar arguments with the customs officers over the export of his antiquities, and arrived back in London early in June.

The general public had come to regard Smith as a sort of archaeological miracle worker, and with good reason judging by his output in the year following his second expedition. Not only did he make a major contribution to the selection of texts for Rawlinson's fourth volume, he wrote and published a popular account of his travels entitled *Assyrian Discoveries*, followed by *The Chaldean Account of Genesis, The*

Assyrian Eponym Canon, Assyria and *Ancient History from the Monuments* as well as preparing the text for *Inscriptions of Sennacherib* and *History of Babylonia* which were not published until some time later. The days when the museum dare not gamble the costs of publication on an unknown young scholar must have seemed very distant.

However, tablets rather than books were Smith's chief aim in life, and in the autumn of 1875 he set off for Istanbul to negotiate another *firman*. On his way he met a young Finnish scholar named Eneberg who was also heading for Nineveh on his government's behalf, and who possessed the additional advantage of knowing some Arabic. It is not surprising that he and Smith struck up a friendship, for they were both equally unfitted by temperament and physique for the rigours of a prolonged sojourn among the Arabs. Even Eneberg's Arabic was not much use, for it was based largely on a study of the Koran and was therefore about as relevant to the demands of everyday life as knowledge of the Talmud would be to conducting business in contemporary Israel.

These two babes in the Oriental wood finally obtained their *firman* in the spring of 1876 and made their way to Aleppo. Here they found that there were two formidable adversaries blocking their way: tribal war in the interior, and an outbreak of cholera. The local people showed rather more sense of self-preservation than the two travellers and refused to risk either themselves or their animals on the road to Mosul. The farthest they could get was a place called Birs Edjik on the Euphrates, and at this point they decided to travel by water to Baghdad as Smith had done on his first expedition. Here they planned to fill in time examining the Babylonian sites until Nineveh should be accessible again. On their arrival Eneberg, who was far from strong, fell ill. Smith could do nothing to help him and in a few days his friend was dead. This personal tragedy did not distract him from the object of his mission. He began to negotiate the purchase of tablets and soon assembled more than 2000.

He finally made his way to Mosul in July, but for all he achieved there he might as well have stayed in the comparative comfort of Baghdad. The people were totally occupied in beating off attacks from sheep-rustling desert nomads. Even without this state of upheaval Smith could not have persuaded them to work for him as they refused pointblank to engage in the exhausting labour of digging in the murderous July heat. The expedition so far had caused Smith so much grief, disappointment and frustration that his last remnant of common sense seems to have deserted him. Turning his back on Mosul he set off precipitately for Aleppo, refusing to wait long enough to acquire proper provisions for the journey or to assemble any supplies of medicine. His lack of necessities was bad enough, but in addition to this he rejected the advice of seasoned travellers who warned him to move only at night and avoid the heat of the day. He had forgotten that his own previous experiences had not included desert conditions in the height of summer.

Under these circumstances the surprising thing is that he managed to get as far as he did, for he was only four days' journey from Aleppo when he finally collapsed, suffering from dysentery aggravated by heat exhaustion and inadequate food. The natives sent a message to the British consul at Aleppo, who hurriedly dispatched medical assistance, but Smith was past help. The doctor managed to transfer him to Aleppo but he was unconscious when he arrived and on 19 August he died. He was only 36 years old.

The *Gilgamesh Epic* was not the end of archaeology's contribution to the story of the Flood. In the 1920s Leonard Woolley undertook a whole series of excavations at Ur of the Chaldees in which he uncovered the dazzling treasures of the Early Dynastic royal burials. Too thorough a scholar to stop here, in 1929 he sank an exploratory pit underneath the royal cemetery to find out what lay in the levels below the tombs. His workman had only gone three feet down when he came to undisturbed earth which he believed to be virgin soil, but Woolley was not satisfied. For one thing it was too near the surface—there should have been many more intervening signs of early occupation—and for another, the earth did not look quite like the soil of the area. Accordingly he set to work next season and carried out further excavations covering a wide area of the ground beneath the cemetery. First he came to eight layers, some six metres deep altogether, of brick debris, and then a further five or so metres of broken pottery, apparently the remains of a series of workshops beginning with the wares of the Jemdet Nasr (protoliterate) period, then the somewhat earlier Uruk wares and finally a few remains dating to the Al 'Ubaid period in the 4th millennium BC.

After these fragments came the empty layer he had noticed the previous year. Three metres deep, it was clean river silt, undisturbed by any sign of human activity or interference. Woolley had specimens analysed, and learned that they were of the same consistency as material deposited from the middle Euphrates area. There it lay, above the earliest Al 'Ubaid levels and the virgin soil, evidence of a massive inundation. While they stared in silent speculation Mrs Woolley strolled over to look. 'Well, of course,' she said, 'It's the Flood.'

The mysterious civilisation of the Indus Valley

The history of archaeology is punctuated, especially in its early days, by a series of points of high drama in which a magnificent work of art or a fabulous treasure bursts upon the dazzled eyes of its discoverer to herald the rapid and comparatively smooth revelation of a hitherto unknown culture to the admiring world. The Indian subcontinent has always been the exception to this as to nearly every other rule; but in view of the conditions with which the archaeological services have had to cope, one can only admire the extent of their achievements. They have to deal with an area considerably larger than Europe but with a far longer cultural history. The climate and geographical setting include the wildest extremes of heat and cold, deluge and desert, mountain and plain, and the land is inhabited by a multitude of different races, languages and religious sects. Invasions have poured over the mountain passes fencing off the north of the subcontinent, each bringing its cultural contribution and taking its toll of the country's resources, and few areas can have been so long subject to the implacable rapacity of resident foreigners who had no interest in or value for any understanding of the traces of ancient and refined civilisation all around them.

Another formidable problem which had to be overcome was the European attitude to archaeology. Right up to the end of the 18th century the phrase 'the ancient world' meant Greek and Roman art. Napoleon's Egyptian campaign extended these boundaries to include the world of the Pharaohs, and the first half of the 19th century saw the awakening of interest in Western Asia, which could be respectably connected with bible studies. But 'native' was still a rude word when applied to people outside Europe and all their past was automatically regarded as inferior to classical or biblical studies. It was not until the second half of the 19th century that it occurred to anyone that Indian culture could be of any serious importance, and even then the study received limited support from officialdom. Curiously enough, one of the most significant Indian civilisations was

also one of the last to be identified and explored.

The first scholar to take a constructive view of Indian culture was Sir Alexander Cunningham, who was appointed Director of Archaeology in 1862 by the Viceroy, Lord Curzon. For years he ranged over the subcontinent, sometimes using local transport but more frequently on foot, acquiring in this way an intimate understanding of the terrain and its people which stood him in good stead in the immense task of formulating a systematic study of the culture. Inevitably he could not investigate everything that came to his notice, but the variety and breadth of his achievement is astonishing. It might justifiably be claimed that the Indus valley civilisation was among the very few that he failed to explore.

The official world was not unaware of the existence of at least one Indus city, but it was thoroughly indifferent to its survival. Nowadays, if a site of major archaeological importance is discovered during the course of public works, there is usually such a concerted howl of general indignation that the bulldozers are temporarily halted until an archaeological rescue operation, however brief and inadequate, can be carried out. This was not true in India 100 years ago, for Harappa, one of the two chief centres of the Indus civilisation, was well known to the engineers who were working on the railroad. Far from thinking of preserving the city, they merely regarded it as a heaven-sent source of excellent-quality fired clay bricks for their project, and as a result of their depredations much of the citadel has been damaged beyond repair. Cunningham had in fact picked up a few surface finds in 1868 and noted the presence of some interesting-looking mounds, but he was predominantly concerned with other sites and it was left to one of his successors, Sir John Marshall, to demonstrate the importance of the culture.

In 1920 two of Marshall's colleagues, D. Shani and N. Banerjee, came across some seals which closely resembled Cunningham's earlier finds, and this encouraged Sir John to initiate an extensive investigation of Mohenjo-daro,

opposite One of the few major statues to emerge from the excavation of Mohenjo-daro shows a head and torso of a bearded individual who, judging by his clothing and regalia, must have held a high position in the city. The strange face with its narrow eyes and thick-lipped mouth has an expression of cold arrogance which has been conveyed with great force and economy by the sculptor.
National Museum of India, New Delhi.

Sir Leonard Woolley never conducted any excavations in the Indian sub-continent, but his advance planning contributed much to the ultimate success of the programme. Called in because of the great reputation he had acquired during his Western Asiatic researches, he drew up a masterly list of suggested reform and a future plan of action to bring some order and system to the chaos into which Indian archaeological studies had fallen.

the other major Indus city, beginning in 1921. His work revealed an astonishingly widespread culture dating at least to the transitional period between the stone and metal ages known as Chalcolithic and on into the Bronze Age, and extending throughout the Indus valley, with centres at Harappa and Mohenjo-daro, 650 kilometres away to the south-west. This civilisation was not Marshall's chief interest–he spent the largest percentage of his time on the Indo-Greek site of Taxila–but he still managed to show that it was geographically the largest in the ancient pre-classical world and that its contacts and influences spread far beyond its own frontiers.

Marshall's excavations, conducted intermittently between 1921 and his retirement in 1929, put the Indus valley firmly on to the archaeological map–but they left a lot of questions unanswered and produced a number of puzzling ambiguities. The entire nature of the civilisation seemed to be different from all its known contemporaries in the ancient world. Where the kingdoms of Egypt and Mesopotamia were embattled military states always engaged in wars of conquest or defence, hag-ridden by superstition and with little choice between priestly, royal and military despotism, there was no trace of any such system to be seen in the Indian subcontinent. Instead of the massive stone and polished marble buildings of the Mediterranean and Western Asiatic kingdoms, the Indus cities were characterised by the unvarying use of excellent kiln-fired bricks which gave them an air of sturdy bourgeois comfort. In addition to this, the early excavations produced no remains of temples, palaces or fortifications. Few weapons and no evidence of the glorification of martial feats were found, and taken together all this suggested an idyllic state of democratic harmony and general peace. Their prosperity in terms of international trade was attested by the discovery of Indus seals as far afield as Ur, Sumer and Tell Asmar in Mesopotamia, and the Akkadian and Sumerian cuneiform documents describe a delightful eastern land, source of timber, precious stones, ivory, 'fish-eyes' (possibly pearls) and other luxury goods which many scholars believe to be the Indus valley.

This view of the civilisation persisted during Marshall's excavations and for a considerable time after his retirement, for there was nothing to modify it–a fact which stressed the great archaeologist's one major shortcoming. He was constitutionally unable to delegate, preferring to centralise all authority and knowledge in himself. As a consequence, when he retired there was no one left with anything like the stature or the experience to take over, and as there had been no training programme worth mentioning this state of affairs could only get worse as time

went on. Not long before the Second World War the Archaeological Service had descended to such a nadir of chaos and inefficiency that it became obvious that outside help was essential, and they sent for Sir Leonard Woolley, perhaps the most eminent European archaeologist of that time, with a request to examine the situation and report on steps needed to rectify it.

Coming as he did from his ordered and scholarly excavations at Carcemish and Ur, with their well-documented background and the organised support of the great universities, learned societies and museums, the problems of India must have seemed (as indeed they were) overwhelming. Starting from scratch, Woolley had to provide recommendations on the basis of which a course of action could be taken to establish archaeological work in a country which had perhaps fewer archaeologists and more ancient remains than most others. Sweeping reforms were needed, and there was little money and no trained staff to carry them out.

Woolley's report was designed to answer four questions, some fairly obvious and others more complex with endless ramifications. First he had to suggest which sites were most likely to be productive of results, so as to avoid wastage of severely limited resources. Next he had to pinpoint the institutions and methods which could most rapidly be developed into efficient archaeological bodies; then he had to draw up a recruitment and training programme. The last and certainly the most far-reaching section offered ideas which might be useful and were not already included under the first three headings. Woolley spent a few strenuous months in India, at the end of which he presented a masterly report which made a fundamental attack on the problems and abuses of Indian archaeology. It was some years before the report could be implemented, for unfortunately there can hardly have been a worse time for initiating a radical reform programme. It was dated 28 February 1939.

When the war in Europe was approaching its climax the Indian government realised that action could be postponed no longer. In the intervening time there had been a great upsurge of national consciousness and the Indians would much have preferred to be the architects of their own archaeological reform; but it was generally if reluctantly recognised that an experienced outsider would be needed to implement the programme. The man they wanted was otherwise engaged at the time, but in February 1944, El Alamein and the Salerno landings safely behind him, Brigadier (later Sir) Mortimer Wheeler left Europe to take up a four-year appointment. In the course of this, he was to reorganise the whole field of Indian archaeology and in the process to clear up many, though by no means all, of the mysteries surrounding the Indus valley civilisation. He describes with obvious relish the impact of his arrival on the torpid functionaries of the moribund Archaeological Survey. However, there must have been a considerable reservoir of untapped talent and enthusiasm, for in an amazingly short time he had assembled a dedicated following of trainees who were quick to learn and happy to follow anywhere he might lead, albeit somewhat appalled at the pace he set.

Most of his time was necessarily devoted to reorganisation work, but much of this was conducted in the field, and it was one such expedition which led to the new insights on the Indus valley cultures. What was meant to be a routine two-hour inspection of the mound at Harappa turned into a day-long improvised excavation which completely reversed established thinking on the nature of the civilisation within the course of six hours' work, or perhaps even in the first ten minutes' observation. As soon as he looked at the mound he realised that it was not a peacefully hospitable city centre but a formidably defended fortress.

Sir Mortimer's original four-year contract was interrupted and saddened by the violence and bloodshed accompanying Partition in 1948, and after this, of course, it was no longer possible for Hindu and Muslim trainees and scholars to work together on the sites and in the universities and museums; but both during the course of his contract and for a few years afterwards he returned from time to time to the Indus valley where his work and that of his successors answered many questions about the civilisation – and raised almost as many more.

It was found that the culture covered an

Sir Mortimer Wheeler, who was chosen to implement Woolley's plan, worked in the sub-continent from 1944 until it became independent in 1948, and made several subsequent visits at the invitations of the various governments. The archaeology of the Indus cultures owes as much to his energy and decision in organising and administration as it does to his encyclopaedic scholarship.

enormously wide area stretching from the Arabian Sea to the Himalayas. The exact limits of its north–south extent are still not entirely clear. In nearly every site two typical characteristics appeared: orderly town planning and the use of fired brick construction work. Almost alone in the ancient world of that date, the Indus towns had a strong feeling for civic decency and order. The town of Mohenjo-daro was seen to be laid out in the regular grid of long avenues and narrower cross-streets set at right angles which is usually associated with Hellenistic and Roman town planning, and this feature can be traced at most of the other Indus sites (Harappa is too badly damaged for the plan to be clear, but there are signs of a similar lay-out). In ancient times Mohenjo-daro lay much closer to the Indus, a proximity which occasionally proved dangerous judging from signs of flooding in low-lying areas, while Harappa lies beside the Ravi, a tributary of the Indus in the Punjab.

The interior planning of the houses gives an impression of comfortable middle-class prosperity, with their central courtyard off which the rooms open so as to give the maximum light and ventilation with the minimum exposure to the noise and dust of the street. They often include a bathroom and a latrine connected to the civic drainage system which is such an outstanding feature of all these towns. Practically every street has its drain, a neatly constructed channel lined and capped with fired bricks and provided with holes for inspection at suitable intervals. Public wells and shelters for watchmen also attest an unusual degree of concern for sanitation and good order seldom seen in the 3rd millennium BC. While such palaces as that of Knossos in Crete, for example, enjoyed a remarkably high standard of plumbing, there is no evidence that the ordinary Minoan towns-folk shared these advantages, as they clearly did in the Indus valley at a substantially earlier date.

Overlooking the tidy chequered pattern of the streets was the citadel, an imposing man-made mound some 15 metres high with forti-fications round it and guard towers at intervals, and here some of the most intriguing structures in the city were uncovered. There were several buildings of an apparently ritual function which made up for the conspicuous absence of any definitely identifiable temples in the town below. These complexes seemed to underline the citizens' preoccupation with cleanliness, for they consisted of a huge tank or bath and a number of smaller baths, each set about with a group of living quarters and cells which sug-

gested a residential priesthood to preside over ritual ablutions. The Great Bath itself measured 11.8 metres by 7 and, like everything else, was chiefly built of baked bricks. Even the best quality terracotta is porous, so the tank and the steps leading down into it were finished with a coat of bitumen to render them waterproof. It was surrounded by balconied rooms and behind it was a deep well-shaft which must have pro-vided water for the bath.

Probably the most remarkable building on the citadel—and another feature which was common to the chief Indus towns—was identi-fied by Sir Mortimer during his work at Mohenjo-daro in 1950. It had puzzled excavators for some time before, and no one had so far been able to think of an explanation for its peculiarities. Its base was a high brick podium with a carefully designed approach and a plat-

For many years a myth persisted of a peaceful nation, undisturbed by threat of violence. This was only dispelled by the discovery at Mohenjo-daro of a formidable citadel. Built of kiln-fired brick, so much stronger and long-lived than sun-dried, it towers threaten-ingly over the lower town, its height enhanced by the stupa of the Buddhist monastery erected on top of it in the 2nd century AD.

form stretching along one side. It seemed to be pierced by a number of open channels of brick, and above it were traces of a huge barn-like structure built mainly of timber. It was obviously not designed as a fort (one does not go to so much trouble to provide easy access to one's defensive centre), it had none of the amenities which might have suggested a palace, and even that useful archaeological stand-by, a temple, did not appear to fit this case in any way. Sir Mortimer and his team toiled for some time among the brick dust and heat in unrelieved perplexity. There was no spectacular find to provide the answer; indeed, Sir Mortimer was not even on the site when it came to him that the wealth of the Indus valley was corn, and the building was the civic granary. The approach was provided so that ox-carts could be led up, the platform along the side was an unloading point, the vents under the timber-work were air ducts to keep the grain fresh and prevent mildew, and the whole complex was designed to meet the needs of an agricultural and mercantile people. The granary was a sort of national bank in the days before coinage, and no doubt tithes were extracted from the populace for storage there.

The slightly anonymous character of the civilisation was perhaps accentuated by its comparative lack of art. Until Sir Mortimer's excavations the best-known works of Indus art had been the seal-stones which were found in large numbers throughout the region and in trade centres far afield. Some of these were of an outstandingly high order of workmanship. Most were square or oblong, though a few were roughly circular, and the motifs were predominantly animals. A considerable quantity of seals

were added to those already known during the 1950 campaign, and these confirmed the impression of remarkable artistry. The designs, carved with a drill and chisel, are sunk in the surface of the seal so that they would appear in relief when the seal was pressed into any soft substance. The animal motifs give some interesting sidelights into the denizens of the Indus valley in the 3rd millennium; they include rhinoceros, crocodiles, tigers, various types of antelope and an elephant which seems to be wearing some kind of back-cloth. This may perhaps be no more than a touch of decorative surface treatment, but if not, it is clear evidence that the elephant was already domesticated.

Another curious creature, less easy to identify, clearly belongs to some breed of cattle. It has been called the 'unicorn' for lack of a more

At the height of its prosperity Mohenjo-daro was a comfortable town, the citizens of which clearly set great value on civic order and cleanliness. The houses were arranged in broad avenues intersected at right-angles by cross-streets, all supplied with efficient and well-maintained drainage systems.

pages 102–103 For many years no sign of any religious buildings were found in association with the Indus Valley sites. Then excavations on the citadel at Mohenjo-daro revealed a curious complex. Although it was not a temple it clearly had a sacred function, probably connected with ritual purification. Flights of steps led down into a great bath, around which were rooms apparently designed for a college of priests.

Beyond the residential quarter of Mohenjo-daro stood the citadel, raised on an artificial mound of bricks out of the reach of potential enemies and the frequent flooding of the Indus river. Within the fortified area stood the only religious building to be identified with any certainty, a large bath-house for ritual ablutions.

opposite top The earliest decorated pottery is usually patterned with little more than a few straight lines. As soon as pictorial representations are attempted, the subject is very often an animal – either the prey of the hunter or the domesticated herds on which survival frequently depended. Pottery fragments from the Indus Valley combine linear decoration with an elegantly stylised long-horned creature carried out in dark painting on a light ground. National Museum of Pakistan, Karachi.

opposite bottom Among the most sophisticated and certainly the most intriguing artifacts of Mohenjo-daro were the square seals with their animal motifs and signs in a still-undeciphered script. A surprising variety of species are shown with a wealth of naturalism in the detail which combines curiously with the occasional appearance of a purely fabulous monster or crudely stylised human being among the familiar domesticated animals. National Museum of India, New Delhi.

The town of Harappa, some 650 kilometres north-east of Mohenjo-daro, was no less important in the Indus Valley culture. Its remains, however, have suffered far more extensively, for it was first located more than a century ago during the construction of a railway, and was merely regarded as a heaven-sent source of excellent quality fired bricks. These depredations did considerable damage, but enough survives to show that it must have been a major city.

accurate term of reference, since only one horn is shown, but this is probably due to the artist's problem with perspective when he had to show one horn behind the other. It always seems to be accompanied by an oddly shaped post which may be a manger. Perhaps the handsomest seal from Mohenjo-daro is a square example showing a truly magnificent humped bull. Accurately observed and perceptively portrayed, the animal is given such importance as to suggest that it was of great value in the Indus society.

Most of the seals bear another motif which has set one of archaeology's most persistent and tantalising problems. There are curious signs engraved alongside the animals which recognisably belong to a script and which therefore lift the Indus culture from the prehistoric to the proto-literate category. No texts have been found and the only other place the signs occur is on pottery and sherds, so it was clearly not a highly developed literary form. Its regular inclusion on seals suggests that these bear the names of the owner, though a religious or amuletic invocation cannot be ruled out. A number of scholars have attempted to decipher

the signs, so far without success. Although they are contemporary with the writing of Egypt and Mesopotamia and the cultures had fairly close commercial contacts, the signs bear no resemblance to the hierglyphic or cuneiform scripts, and until the present they have defied every attempt to penetrate their meaning, including the most modern application of computer analysis.

The human race fares considerably less well than the animals on the seals. The first motif produced by mankind when he becomes an artist is usually the animal which he hunts, but he is by nature inclined to be narcissistic and once he is no longer dependent on animal prey for survival one of the images he has always made with great pleasure is his own. In fact, only the severest religious prohibitions ever prevent him from doing so, and as a general rule the walls of his palaces, shrines and homes are ornamented chiefly with representations of the human form. From long practice and instinctive understanding of his subject the artist usually achieves mastery over this motif and learns to use it to express his preoccupations. This does not seem to be true of the Indus people, for on the rare

occasions when human figures are shown on the seals they are crude and stylised, the details unresolved and the whole conception expressing little but a consuming lack of interest in the subject. This impression is reinforced by the comparative absence of human representations in the buildings of Harappa and Mohenjo-daro.

When they do occur, however, Indus carvings of the human figure show enormous divergence of artistic ability and sophistication. In a stone torso from Harappa with dowel holes for the attachment of limbs the modelling is so sensitive and the delicately balanced curve of the turning body so finely controlled that it would not be out of place in Hellenistic Greece. Unfortunately it is impossible to establish with any certainty that the piece dates to the Indus period (it may be slightly later) and the other surviving sculptures are by no means always of the same calibre. The terracotta mother-goddess figures with their elaborate head-dresses and jewellery are so simplified as to be almost childish, with no technique beyond joining a few rolls and blobs of clay together, and the strange grotesques exhibit more sense of humour than artistry. Clay caricatures, they show fat women, weird pig-men and a goggle-eyed person with an enormous tongue hanging out. A terracotta bull and the head of a tiger, perhaps a cat, are notably superior in both conception and execution.

There are only two pieces which redeem Indus human figure sculpture, and they appear to represent opposite ends of the social scale. One of them is clearly a personage of high position and authority. The nature of his rank is unknown, but whatever it was he looks as if he did not exercise it with benevolence. All that survives is the head and torso of a man wearing a fillet round his head and a simply-cut robe, worn over one shoulder and under the other, of cloth decorated with a trefoil pattern. The trefoils have raised outlines which suggest some kind of inlay, especially as they also have a pin hole in the middle of each lobe, but there is no trace left to show what material was used. The man has straight hair fastened in a bun at the nape of his neck and a short beard covers his chin but not his upper lip. The facial type is arresting; the forehead slopes back above the eyes and there is very little back to the head, but it is the expression which is most striking. Narrow lids droop superciliously over long slit eyes and the thick-lipped mouth curves down at the outer corners with cold arrogance. If this was the only survivor of the type it would convey a most disagreeable impression of the Indus hierarchy, but fortunately there are two other heads of the same kind with pleasant, even smiling features. Most dynasties have their unacceptable face, and the Indus sculpture has not been afraid strongly to characterise one of them.

The other outstanding example of sculpture could hardly be a greater contrast. It is a small bronze figure of a dancing girl, nude except for a necklace and an armful of bracelets. She has the same narrow eyes and thick mouth, and wears her hair drawn back and coiled into a rope lying on one shoulder. The underdeveloped body indicates youth but both her pose and her expression are redolent of experience. One hip is thrown out with her hand resting on it, her

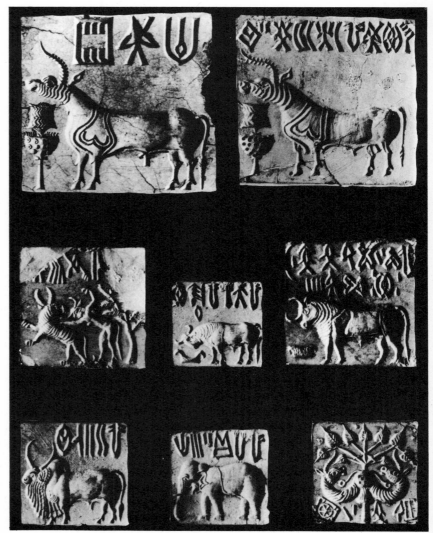

chin is lifted and her head tilted so that her long-lidded eyes shoot provocative sidelong glances. This sympathetic study implies that it was much more fun to be a member of the lower orders in Mohenjo-daro.

One of the many mysteries of the Indus culture is its date. 'Chalcolithic' is a technological rather than a chronological description – after all, there were plenty of pre-metal cultures still active in the 20th century – and it is therefore not possible to assume that the culture is necessarily contemporary with others at the same technical stage of development. Carbon-14 tests suggested a rough dating of 2500–1500 BC which was confirmed by the Indus seals found in more securely dated Mesopotamian contexts. However, no one had managed to explore the site of Mohenjo-daro right down to virgin soil to see if anything could be learned about the origins of the culture, and in 1950 Sir Mortimer Wheeler decided to make a determined effort to get, literally, to the bottom of the site. His observations during the excavation proved

that the level of the land had risen year by year because of the silt deposited in the spring floods of the Indus, and as this process took place the water table beneath the surface had risen correspondingly. Previous attempts to dig through the occupation levels to virgin soil had been foiled by the water, so Sir Mortimer brought pumps to cope with the seepage and set to work. The trenches were already formidably deep, and they had to dig a further five metres or so before they hit the water level. All available labour was mobilised to bale and man the pumps, and they managed to push on for a further three metres. The seepage had now turned into jets of water spurting from all sides of the cutting and there was still no sign of virgin soil. Overnight the trench turned into a well and they knew they were beaten.

The end of the civilisation, although more accessible to archaeological investigation than the beginning, is still disputed. A great culture extending over an immensely large area does not suddenly switch off all at once, and there are many hints that it was in a stage of decline long before the end came. As one layer of houses fell or was pushed down the new ones built on top of the levelled surface were increasingly less solid and well constructed. Town planning gradually lapsed and the trim streets and avenues degenerated into an untidy urban muddle. There was no single reason for this; many different elements probably contributed. A whole city built of fired bricks, which were essential to stand up to the Indus floods, must have needed untold millions of bricks over the course of centuries and timber cutting for the kilns must have denuded the land dangerously. Possibly the malarial mosquito played a part, or perhaps the fertility of the vital grain lands suffered in a series of natural disasters in addition to the deforestation caused by the inhabitants. Certainly there are signs of increasing and abnormal flooding in the later levels of the Indus cities.

Whatever the cause, prosperity declined sharply and when the invaders came – whoever they were – the Indus people were burned out and too enfeebled to put up much resistance. The invaders evidently did not want to live in Mohenjo-daro themselves, for they left the unburied dead lying where they had fallen in numbers which would soon have made any hot-climate town uninhabitable. The most recent excavators have found skeletons scattered about the streets in attitudes eloquently suggestive of violent death. One group of 14 had evidently been cornered in a room where men, women and children were slaughtered. The town was thoroughly sacked, very little of value escaping the attention of the looters, and fires broke out here and there among the abandoned

Many civilisations have a tendency in their formative stages to practise a domestic fertility cult based on mother-goddess figurines. The Indus Valley was no exception, and a number of small clay figures of the mother have been found. The workmanship is crude and the forms stylised, stressing the sexual characteristics which symbolised fertility and the masses of elaborate jewellery which was meant to ensure wealth. National Museum of Pakistan, Karachi.

buildings. If there were any survivors they were unable, or too frightened, to come back and give decent burial to their massacred fellow townsmen.

Pockets of the culture lingered on in various sites throughout the Indus valley, but the newcomers (Indra and the Aryans are the favourite candidates for this role) were soon firmly entrenched and the last remnants of the old life style gradually died out.

In the hundred years or so of its existence the archaeology of the Indus cultures has solved a large number of fascinating problems, but in the course of the investigations almost as many more have been raised. The origins of the culture are still to seek, the script is still undeciphered, the social structure and religion of the people are unknown and it has so far been impossible to establish how or even exactly when it came to an end. Perhaps future studies will throw more light on these questions, but in the meantime the Indus valley civilisation remains one of archaeology's enigmas.

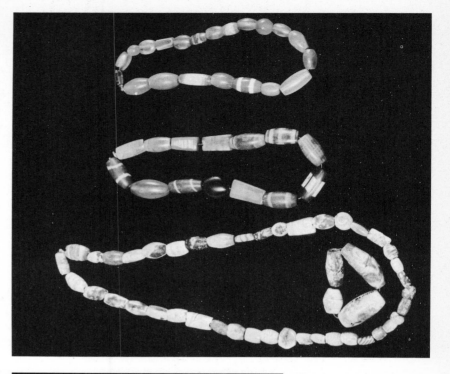

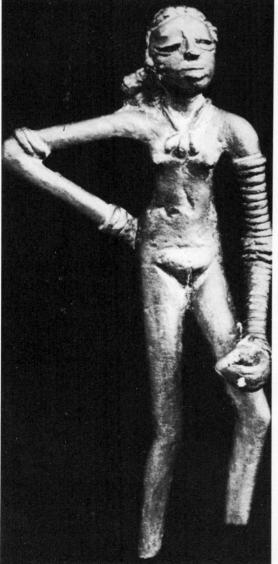

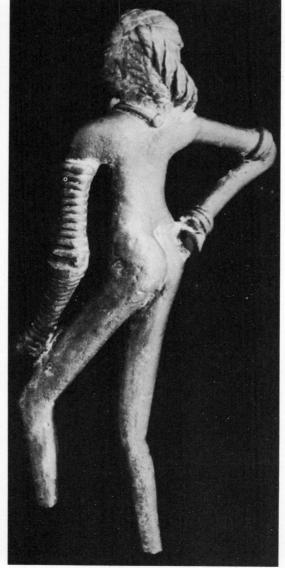

The invaders who finally destroyed Mohenjo-daro looted the site with a thoroughness which left little in the way of treasure or works of art for the later excavators to find. A small hoard found in the lower city managed to escape the plunderers, and proved that the Indus peoples, like most others, were fond of ornaments, and wore a wide variety of different stones drilled for necklaces.
National Museum of Pakistan, Karachi.

Undoubtedly one of the most attractive, certainly the most sexy, works of art from the Indus Valley is a bronze statuette of a young dancing girl, nude except for her plentiful jewellery. She shows the same type of features as the stone figure of a ruler (p. 96) but here the long-lidded eyes shoot inviting sidelong glances, the thick mouth has a sensual curve and the pert pose, one hand poised on an out-thrust hip, is redolent of provocative confidence.

Jericho:
the first city dwellers

'The romance of archaeology' is a phrase which seems to occur fairly frequently in accounts of the great 19th-century discoveries. There was some justice in the description, for at this time many of these explorations were conducted under extraordinarily romantic circumstances. An intrepid traveller, alone or accompanied by a native guide who could be relied on only to be totally unreliable, would vanish into the jungle or the desert and after undergoing numerous colourful hardships and hazards, return with news of a brilliant find. Most of the subsequent excavations would be carried out with no help but that of a force of unmanageable and capricious local labour, many miles from 'civilisation' and far beyond the reach of competent assistance should any emergency arise. From these distant locations evidence would emerge to set the world of letters in a buzz of excitement. Reports of noble temples and palaces would be backed up with examples of sculptures and paintings, gold and jewels, bronzes and ivories, and sometimes inscriptions relating the history behind the artifacts, and finally the explorer himself would return to tell his story in a best-selling book and innumerable crowded public lectures.

Archaeology has changed a great deal since its heroic age in the last century. However, the romance is still there, though it wears a very different aspect today. The contemporary archaeologist's incentive lies in extending the frontiers of knowledge and uncovering the truth about the formative years of the human race, not by means of discoveries as sudden and spectacular as exploding fireworks, but by the application of meticulous scientific methods. There are no more solo expeditions into inaccessible places by an explorer armed with a bedding-roll, a spade and a vague notion that he might find something interesting. No one undertakes a campaign unless they are already as sure as one reasonably can be of where they are going to dig and what they are going to find, because a modern excavation, although it seldom includes the perils and vicissitudes of former times, is a highly complex operation.

A typical example of modern trends in excavation and archaeological discovery was the dig conducted by Dr (now Dame) Kathleen Kenyon at Jericho in the early 1950s. The enormous mound in the Jordan valley, just to the north of the Dead Sea, had been attracting scholarly attention for nearly a century because of its connections with the Old Testament story of Joshua, but Dr Kenyon's work was destined to illuminate the much broader question of the foundations of civilisation itself. The exact definition of the beginning of civilisation is a question which has occupied a great deal of semantic, philosophical and sociological debate, but as a working hypothesis it might perhaps be described as the time when man stopped living in isolated units with every man for himself – or at the most for himself and his immediate family group – and came together to live in permanent towns with an organised social structure and some ideas beyond the immediate basic necessities of procuring enough food and shelter. For many years it was believed that this movement first manifested itself significantly in Egypt and southern Mesopotamia around the 4th or 5th millennium BC, and that it was characterised by the development of pottery and the beginnings of literacy. Dr Kenyon's excavation pushed back these boundaries dramatically by proving the existence of a considerable town with a high level of community organisation long before the appearance of writing or even of pottery, in at least the 7th millennium BC.

These conclusions were gradually formed in the course of four years' digging, by piecing together innumerable seemingly insignificant scraps of information until a clear picture emerged. The dig was a ponderous operation. Once the investigation of Jericho had been decided upon, permission had to be obtained from the authorities of the Hashemite Kingdom of Jordan, and an agreement reached about the division of any possible finds from the dig. Local landowners had to be suitably appeased, and an excavation team assembled for which, inevitably, considerable sums of money were

opposite Most of the plaster-coated skulls from Jericho have lost the lower jaw, which spoils the proportion of the re-modelled head. The finest surviving example, however, is intact, and shows a subtlety and delicacy of treatment which is almost incredible at so early a date, the cowrie shells set into the eye-sockets giving a feeling of sight. These also, incidentally, suggest trading connections with coastal people.

From the beginning of civilisation the dominant factor
in the history of Western Asia has been water, the rare
and precious necessity of desert lands. The Jericho
spring can legitimately claim to be older than civilisation,
for it was here that the earliest settlers were attracted
to establish their town and lay out their fields more than
9000 years ago; and here the women still bring their
traditionally shaped water-pots, just as they always did.

The Jericho excavations overturned many predetermined ideas about the earliest stages of human urban development. The massive walls built by the Neolithic people indicate that theirs was not an isolated example of advanced culture. Such defences as these were intended to keep out something far more formidable than the occasional tribe of wandering nomads; enemies at least as powerful as themselves must have been anticipated.

opposite The vast mound of Jericho has for decades been a focus of attention for biblical scholars. Early – but not the earliest – on the site were German teams of 1908–11, some of whose work is shown here. Unfortunately, most excavators started off their work with a rigidly preconceived picture of what they would find: the walls that fell down at the sound of Joshua's trumpets. Because of this preoccupation, many highly important aspects of the site were neglected until it came to be investigated by an entirely open-minded and objective team who set out to find out what was there rather than to support an existing hypothesis.

needed. A single body is seldom able to supply the funds for all the personnel and equipment of a modern campaign, and Dame Kathleen lists her sponsors as the British School of Archaeology in Jerusalem, the Palestine Exploration Fund and the British Academy. Help, subsidies and co-operation were also provided by the American School of Oriental Research, the Royal Ontario Museum of Toronto, the Russel Trust, Sydney University, Birmingham City Museum, the Ashmolean Museum, the Australian Institute of Archaeology, Oxford University Committee for Advanced Studies, Cambridge University Museum of Archaeology and Ethnology, the Universities of Liverpool, London, Leeds, Manchester, Nottingham, Durham, Glasgow, Reading, Edinburgh, Emory (Georgia), Leiden, Trinity Colleges Dublin and Cambridge, Queen's College, Oxford, Leeds City Museum and the Royal Anthropological Institute, among others. A tremendous effort of organisation must have been needed simply to co-ordinate so many disparate bodies.

The next requirement was a trained staff. Non-professionals can still make an invaluable contribution when they work under proper supervision, but the day of the inspired amateur is over, and the Jericho enterprise called for a large team of experts. In addition to Dr Kenyon there were, throughout the course of the dig, 54 field supervisors, 3 photographers, 4 technical assistants, 3 draughtsmen, a Registrar and her 6 assistants, 4 anthropologists, 4 camp supervisors, a journalist and a number of visiting experts, all of whom required transport, equipment, supplies and somewhere to work and live at Jericho from January to April each season from 1952 to 1956.

Jericho owes its survival for nearly 9000 years to the existence of an abundant freshwater spring which supports a welcoming green oasis in the glaring arid lowlands of the Jordan valley. People were attracted to this spring at a very early date, and had little incentive to leave it, so they settled down, established farms and grazing lands and built a town with walls to defend their homes against other wanderers in the area. As generations and centuries passed the town overflowed its limits, not only outwards but upwards. Houses grew shabby and shaky, and new inhabitants knocked them down, levelled the rubble and built again on top, sealing the debris and any abandoned objects underneath in an archaeological layer-cake which finally reached a height of over 20 metres. These mounds (or *tells*, to give them their local name) are common all over western Asia, and the records of the past preserved in each layer can be 'read' by anyone with the skill and knowledge to cut a vertical slice through from top to bottom and study the exposed layers.

Here, however, the cake analogy ends. The layers are not regular, flat and homogeneous, the same thickness wherever they occur, but uneven, changing consistency from one point to another, sometimes petering out altogether. Nor can one ever be certain that everything in any given layer belongs to the same date, for later inhabitants often dug pits for one reason or another which penetrated into the level below so that in this place the levels become confused, with later material at the bottom of the pit in association with the earlier level, and occasional remains from this date thrown up to the level of the later inhabitants while they were in the process of digging the pit. The best way to keep a check on these irregularities is to sink a number of trenches of carefully measured size and shape, with sides as smooth and flat as possible, on which the levels can be seen reasonably clearly and traced from point to point.

The old technique of stripping off the layers horizontally from the top is seldom used, as it destroys all the recent layers in the process of reaching the lower ones. On a *tell* like Jericho where the main trench was 15.24 metres deep this method presented considerable technical problems, but it was the only one which would preserve the record of the successive occupants in their chronological relationship to each other. This was essential, for it could justifiably be claimed that most finds are of little value or importance in themselves and only become significant when seen in the context of their position in the excavation. It has been claimed that an object moved is, in archaeological terms, an object destroyed unless careful drawings, photographs and measurements have been taken first, whence comes the golden rule for amateurs: if you stumble across a find, send for an expert and, above all, do not touch it.

The Jericho dig embodied all the usual difficulties of a large-scale excavation and a great many more. A permit to conduct the excavation was no problem as the mound belonged to the government; but accommodation for the site personnel had to be negotiated afresh each year with the local landowners, taking into account all the ramifications of joint ownership and sub-leasing which could be both nebulous and obstructive but always seemed to cost more in the end. Staff was simpler; most of the archaeologists were imported, with the exception of a few Jordanian experts, but manual labour was recruited locally. The inhabitants of modern Jericho were desperately poor and the prospect of up to 200 jobs digging and removing earth must have been more than welcome. The rates of pay started at two shillings a day for a little boy and rose through two shillings and sixpence for a big boy and three shillings for an unskilled man to the splendid height of five shillings for a

A BYZANTINE URN

A CANAANITE JUG

ANOTHER SPECIMEN OF CANAANITE WARE

A DRINKING-CUP

AN ISRAELITE JAR

ANOTHER SPECIMEN OF ISRAELITE POTTERY

THE OUTER WALLS OF JERICHO, EXCAVATED BY THE GERMANS

CANAANITE POTSHERDS

CANAANITE HOUSES BEHIND THE INNER WALLS OF THE CITADEL

CANAANITE POTSHERDS

Last week we illustrated the wonderful discoveries which the Germans have made on the site of Babylon. On this page, by the courtesy of the German Oriental Society, we are enabled to show some results of their recent excavations at Jericho, where they have brought to light remains of the various civilisations which occupied the famous site from 2000 B.C. The most important discovery, after the walls of Jericho, was the ancient citadel with the adjoining Canaanite houses on the northern slopes of the city. At five different spots flights of stone steps were found. In addition to specimens of ancient Canaanite ware, numerous domestic utensils were discovered bearing a close relationship to Greco-Phœnician pottery, and a number of graves of the early Byzantine era, containing urns and other vessels, were also uncovered.

skilled man. Inevitably there was a certain amount of argument as to which category each worker belonged to, but on the whole they were only too glad of the work, and many attained a high degree of skill and usefulness which increased every year as they returned to the dig for the season.

Planning the actual assault on the mound was complicated by the activities of earlier excavators who had not worked within the framework of a carefully ordered system. The first shafts were sunk there in 1865 by a team of Royal Engineers operating under the sponsorship of the Palestine Exploration Fund. After digging a six-metre trench into the south side of the *tell* they decided there was nothing of interest to be learned, and abandoned the site. Digging was not resumed until 1908–11 when a team of Austrians and Germans conducted some meticulous investigations. They did the best they could, but the knowledge, especially of pottery dating, available at that time was insufficient to enable them to reach any conclusions which have stood the test of time. The first well-grounded excavations were those of Professor John Garstang, from 1930 to 1936. He was chiefly interested in Joshua's Jericho, hunting assiduously for the walls which traditionally came tumbling down at the blast of the Israelite general's trumpets, but even with the improved knowledge of his day Garstang's work obviously needed much expansion and correction, and the

Kenyon campaigns were designed to carry this out.

The first step was to make a cutting into the side of the mound to establish the sequence of strata, and this was most easily done by continuing Garstang's main trench. They began by digging through the modern debris on the top of the *tell*. After this they came to a small area of Late Bronze Age, then Middle Bronze Age remains, followed by the Amorite level. Then came the Early Bronze Age remains just above the evidence of a Neolithic people who used pottery, and finally a thick layer of pre-pottery Neolithic remains resting on undisturbed bedrock. It was this earliest level which produced evidence of the surprising and hitherto unsuspected fact that organised urban communities existed long before the development of pottery.

Early Jericho was no primitive village of mud huts, but a considerable town surrounded by fortifications, and with adequate housing for a large population. Assessments are bound to be speculative, but judging by the analogy of contemporary Near Eastern towns of a similar structure, ancient Jericho may have housed up to 3000 citizens at the height of its prosperity.

The many centuries of habitation before the arrival of pottery-making people were divided into two phases which, between them, produced an accumulation of archaeological debris nearly 14 metres thick. The earliest settlers of all lived in houses made of oddly shaped bricks of

Like so many of his contemporaries, Garstang had to begin his excavation by trying to sort out, identify and bring some order into the efforts of his predecessors. The earliest archaeological excavations at Jericho had been conducted in 1865 by a team of Royal Engineers, whose operations were more redolent of sapping, trenching and mining than scholarly investigation, and their operations provided just one of Garstang's preliminary problems.

Quite apart from the scholastic problems set by its boundless complexity, the tell of Jericho can be notably dangerous on a purely practical level. By the time Garstang began his work there, the system of cutting trenches through the archaeological layers had been established; but Jericho was so vast that these trenches had to be immensely deep. Given sandy soil and a bone-dry atmosphere, the risk of a cave-in could never be ignored, and very little could be done to guard against it.

sun-dried clay, roughly oval in shape with a flat bottom and a hog's-back ridge along the top. This is not a convenient shape for building, and it is difficult to surmise what made the early builders select such an awkward form. Whatever their reason, they used these bricks to build rounded houses with walls that curved inwards like beehives, with a lot of timber in the construction and floors laid over a foundation of cobble stones. They were clearly an agricultural people, from the evidence of the tools and equipment found in this layer, for these include far more farming than hunting implements.

This dependence on cultivation may have been responsible for Jericho's early movement into civic organisation, for the farms could never have survived without a properly controlled distribution of the spring water for irrigation which must have imposed mutually acceptable rules on the community.

Though their life-style was in general so orderly, it included one feature which is surprising in any town situated in a hot climate; the inhabitants usually buried their dead in deep pits under the floors of their homes instead of removing them to a cemetery at a hygienic

distance away from the town. There are, however, indications that there was a superstitious reason behind this practice. They seem to have believed that the wisdom and protection of their forebears could be secured by preserving the dead man's skull. After burial the bodies were left to decompose and after a suitable interval the skull was detached and grouped with others to keep watch over the living. Another religious custom belonging to this age was that of child sacrifice. One building contained a small trough made of mud plaster near which were a number of babies' skulls, the neck vertebrae of which showed clear signs of having been severed.

The people who monopolised the fertile oasis around the spring had plenty to defend and were obviously aware of considerable menace from outside, for at an early date (well before 6800 BC, according to carbon-14 dating) they constructed an impressive series of fortifications which they repaired and reconstructed at intervals throughout their occupation of Jericho. The first thing a putative attacker would meet would have been a huge ditch three metres deep and nine metres wide. This structure, which was early but by no means the earliest defence, was hollowed out of solid bed-rock, and the making of such a ditch with nothing but Neolithic tools must have been a tremendous undertaking. Experiments have shown that one of the most effective methods of working stone

without the advantages of modern cutting edges is simply to hit it with another piece of the same or harder stone until the surplus is knocked away. Another way is to soak the stone thoroughly and then to build a fire against it. The water which has penetrated the surface then turns to steam, expanding in the process and splitting up the stone. This was the method used by local farmers to destroy some of the Stonehenge monoliths before the days of conservation.

Having negotiated the hazards of the ditch the attacker would find himself facing the wall itself. It was built of smallish stones, undressed but carefully selected and combined to form a smooth, regular face which offered little foothold. Inside the wall was a backing of fill on which the defenders could stand. This advantage in height was reinforced by the most spectacular element in Jericho's defences—a massive round tower nine metres in diameter with a staircase of stone slabs in the centre leading down to a mysterious passageway. The stair and the corridor were both finished with big slabs of dressed stone which indicated that they were of great importance, but the excavators were unable to trace the passage to its end, so that they never discovered its precise function. Towards the end of this phase, however, the citizens found an unexpected use for it. When it had filled up with rubble to within less than a metre of the roof twelve dead Jerichoans were

dumped into it, and there the skeletons remained in what can have been no more than a useful rubbish tip by this time.

The invaders who coveted the oasis were evidently successful in the end, and the people using hog's-back bricks vanished, to be followed by a short period when the town was undefended. Clearly it was far too enviable a location to remain open for long, and soon the new people built more defences, re-facing the earlier ones at some points. They adopted (or brought with them) several of their predecessors' ways, but not their clumsy bricks. The newcomers also built their homes of sun-dried clay bricks, but they preferred an oblong shape with a series of little ridged thumb-prints along the top to give the clay mortar a better grip. They succeeded so well in this that the excavators had the utmost difficulty in loosening any single brick from the wall intact. The houses made a surprisingly attractive impression. Even at a considerably later date space was usually the prerogative of the great palace dwellers, and ordinary citizens often lived in cramped little rooms which must have been disagreeably airless and stuffy. At Jericho, however, it was not unusual for rooms to attain the respectable size of seven metres by three with large doorways to allow for free movement of air when the doors were open. Cooking, sensibly enough, was not done indoors. A hearth of smoothed clay was

made in the courtyard with which each house was provided so that the heat, dirt and smells could be kept to the open air. The vicinity of these hearths naturally tended to become rather messy, and when the Jericho housewife's sense of propriety was sufficiently offended she would have the area flattened and a new coat of fresh clay laid on the top. This sometimes happened so often that the level of the courtyard grew noticeably higher than that of the interior and a doorstep had to be installed to keep it where it belonged.

The replastering of the hearths is not the only indication of a feeling for domestic cleanliness. One of the most pleasant features of the typical Jericho house of this era was its floor. This was made of the finest clay that could be obtained, which was then polished by rubbing it with a rounded piece of smooth stone until it was so well burnished that it was nearly waterproof, and could be cleaned by sluicing it down with water. Where these floors met the walls they were curved up to the vertical so that there was no angle where dust and mud could accumulate. These provisions were supplemented by an occasional drain consisting of a sunken channel capped by flat stones in a courtyard, but there was no evidence of a well-developed civic drainage system. No remains of household furniture have survived, apart from built-in stone benches and storage bins, but there are signs that reed mats, both oblong and oval, were woven and laid on the floors, where the imprint of the texture has been preserved.

The stone tools and vessels of these people provided a sketchy picture of their lives. There was a little hunting gear but far more agricultural equipment, the commonest being flint sickle blades with skilfully manufactured saw teeth. Obviously grain was the chief crop, and the basis of Jericho's diet, as confirmed by the grindstones which frequently occurred. The corn was ground by a worker sitting on the edge of an oblong stone block and rubbing the grains with an oval piece of hard stone. These were very useful as they could also function as burnishers for the plaster floors and polishers to put the finishing touches to stone vessels. In fact, there seem to have been few other heavy-duty tools as nothing suggesting picks, hoes, or axes was found.

One of mankind's most persistent instincts is that of vanity, from which the Jerichoans were not immune. There is no evidence to show how they dressed, although the rush mats and the discovery of loom weights indicate that they knew how to weave, but they obviously enjoyed adorning themselves with beads and would go to considerable trouble to obtain these ornaments. Bright green malachite was often strung into necklaces, and cowrie shells, for which they must have traded with coastal settlements, were great favourites.

The social structure of early Jericho is still a mystery. No building has been uncovered which could be identified as a palace and only one which might have a religious significance, although even this is questionable. A few tiny clay female figurines may have been mother-goddesses; but while it is true that people who depend for survival on the continuing reproductive cycle of their fields and herds are apt to set a high value on the female principle, one must be a little wary of such easy interpretations. They may be no more than children's toys. The excavators had similar reservations about the building they tentatively called the 'temple'. It had a large oblong central room with a small basin in the middle, and the polished plaster of the floor showed signs of fire all around the edge of this container. There were curved rooms like apsidal chapels at either end of the oblong chamber. After the manner of archaeologists the world over, they interpreted it as a ritual building because they could think of no other explanation for the oddities of its design and equipment.

Modern field archaeology is a highly disciplined science, and at Jericho a strict adherence to the rules almost obliged the investigators to pass over one of the most intriguing and illuminating discoveries of the entire campaign. It is fundamentally important to keep the walls of

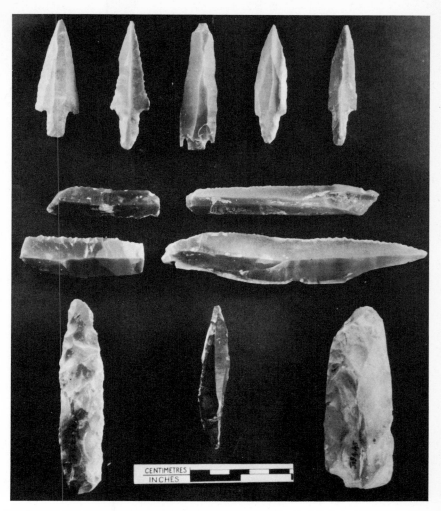

It used to be thought that pottery technology was essential for the development of urban communities with a basically agricultural economy, but Jericho pre-dates the introduction of pottery by many centuries.

The people of Jericho seemed to have made a cult of the human skull, believing perhaps that it ensured the continuing presence of the wisdom and goodwill of the ancestor to whom it had once belonged.

opposite It was impossible to impose an orderly grid system of excavation on the massive confusion of Jericho, so a huge main trench, extending Garstang's original one, was cut towards the heart of the mound. The flat walls of the trench, more than 15 metres high, rise above the remains of the Neolithic walls, ditch and tower in a sheer cliff which suggests something of the hazards of working in these conditions.

trenches as flat and smooth as cutting can make them if the stratigraphy is to be easily and clearly read. This means that one must not go burrowing off into the sides of the trench, no matter what tantalising indications one may see there. In the wall of one of the Jericho trenches was the top of a human skull, and for some time the assistants had been anxious to pick it out of the wall and examine it. Dame Kathleen would not allow this. Human bones were not so rare at Jericho as to make it a find of unique importance and she did not want to spoil her trench for any insignificant reason. The 1955 season drew to its close, and the camp site was being broken up. Most of the technical equipment and the few comforts enjoyed by the team had already been packed up and set away when she finally gave reluctant permission for the skull to be detached, once the strata of the area had been carefully recorded. The ancient, brittle bone presented some difficulties, but as the earth was gently scraped away all round it, they began

to see that it was more than just another skull. The top, which had been the only part visible in the wall of the trench, was bare but the rest of the skull had been coated with fine plaster and remodelled into a semblance of life. What was more, when they lifted it out of the wall they could see that there were others embedded in the soil behind it.

Working with makeshift equipment and living in spartan conditions the excavators spent a week on the demanding task of extracting these fragile objects, but they were amply rewarded by the results. One of these skulls was generally acknowledged to be the most beautiful of them all. It had been fully intact when it was plastered, with its jaw still in place (the others had no lower jaw, which tended to spoil the finished proportions). The plaster had been so sensitively modelled into such fine and delicate features that this object alone proved the high artistic abilities of the Jerichoans beyond a doubt. There were traces of paint which suggested that the finished head had been given a life-like colouring, and cowrie shells had been set in the plaster eye-sockets, the edges of the shell forming the upper and lower lids of half-closed eyes.

Further investigations showed that the skulls had been an important part of life in Jericho. Bodies had been dug up in considerable numbers and ruthlessly dismembered to acquire a suitable cranium for plastering, and the finished piece was clearly a treasured possession. Modern comparisons suggested that they might have been either the skulls of enemies killed in war and preserved as a trophy and a momento of the victors' prowess, or the heads of venerated ancestors. A number of circumstances made the latter possibility seem the most likely. At least 30 skeletons had been rifled to obtain skulls, but none of them showed any trace of the kind of injury which might cause death in battle. It seemed improbable that the people of Jericho would have buried dead enemies under the floors of their own homes, and the practice persisted for so long that one cannot postulate a continual state of war throughout so many decades. Finally there is the evidence, admittedly subjective but none the less valid, of the skulls themselves. They are highly individualised portraits, one of which at least represents an extraordinarily beautiful person. Artistic mentality must have changed a great deal if such love and care and skill were lavished on an enemy. Most of those who studied these heads came to the conclusion that they were kept, like those of the earliest period, to watch over their descendants, and that the semblance of life imparted by the painted plaster preserved the living qualities of the departed for the benefit and protection of those who came after.

The skulls were archaeologically important

The Jericho dig was conducted chiefly in the early months of the year. There is no season when the area can offer cool, fresh conditions, and labour in the airless trenches was extraordinarily demanding. The remains with which the excavators were dealing were of such great age that the utmost skill and care was needed to handle them. Objects like the child's skeleton shown here might disintegrate at a touch if wrongly handled.

not only because of the light they shed on early cult practices but because they indicated a level of artistry which was not apparent anywhere else on the site. They were, however, almost the only find from Jericho which could have provoked any excitement or interest in the general public. For the most part the excavation was a matter of disciplined hard work extending over several years during which innumerable fragments of information were painstakingly collected and patiently collated. The results may not have had the immediate visual appeal of, say, the Assyrian palaces at Nineveh or the noble Greek cities of Asia Minor, but Jericho's contribution to knowledge of the past is probably far greater than these glamorous excavations.

At a date within three millennia of the ending of the last Ice Age when, it used to be believed, men were poor primitive troglodytes, barely emerging from their wretched caves, the people of Jericho were living in a fine city which could have compared favourably with many medieval centres as far as its domestic appointments and military installations were concerned. In addition the results of the excavation produced implications reaching far beyond the actual site of the city. If the people had to build such massive fortifications they obviously had to defend themselves against an enemy far more formidable than a few wandering nomads. The imported materials which cannot have been obtained from local sources indicate trade contacts with other people who were sufficiently well established to have a surplus available for commercial dealings. It is clear, therefore, that the city of Jericho, the oldest known town in the world, cannot have been unique, but although other ancient towns are known nothing comparable has ever been found belonging to such an early date. This is a case where archaeology has shed a fascinating new light on the past, and, at the same time, pointed a possibly fruitful direction for future studies and investigations.

When the pottery levels of Jericho were reached they presented a new problem of organisation. Thousands upon thousands of broken sherds (the excavators seldom had the pleasure of an intact piece) had to be unearthed with all due precautions, cleaned, recorded, stored and all the circumstances of their discovery logged in meticulous detail. A special shed, shown here, was set aside for this exacting but essential task.

Tutankhamun: the boy king

On 11 July 1881 a small steam-launch was moving down the Nile, at the centre of a strange procession. From the countryside on either bank came *fellahin*, the men loosing salvoes of rifle-fire while the women tore their hair as they raised the wailing lament for a dead king. Their cry can seldom have been more appropriate, for the boat was loaded with the mummies of 40 of the greatest rulers in Egypt's immemorial history. Centuries ago they had been laid to rest in their magnificent tombs in the Valley of the Kings, with solemn ceremony and unimaginable treasures of gold and jewels. Few, if any, people have ever believed quite so literally as the ancient Egyptians in the material truth of resurrection. The status and the life-style of a dead man in the next world depended entirely on the goods that were buried with him, and resurrection would be impossible if his physical body had not been preserved for his spirit to reoccupy. Life was one long preparation for death and eternity, and the splendour of one's funeral appointments reflected one's position in life and hopes for hereafter. In the case of the pharaohs and their consorts, whose power and wealth were limitless, the reality of these provisions surpassed in their fabulous splendour all the golden imaginings of myth and legend.

Such magnificence carried the seeds of its own destruction; it is doubtful if there has ever before or since been so totally irresistible an incentive to robbery. Every possible precaution was taken to prevent it. The tombs, constructed by as few workers as possible, were honeycombed with false passages and pits to trap the unwary, divine protection was invoked in carved and painted formulae, the entrances were disguised and hidden, and watch was kept day and night by the guards and priests of the Theban necropolis. Hideous penalties awaited the thief in this world, and damnation in the next, but with such rewards to be won all these measures were doomed to failure. Every known royal grave, including that of Tutankhamun, was entered by robbers within weeks, sometimes within hours of the burial, and that of Tutan-khamun was the only one to escape extensive depredation.

Most vulnerable of all, perhaps because they were the richest, were the mighty pharaohs of the New Kingdom dynasties. Egypt's power abroad and prosperity at home were at their height in this era, and the necropolis authorities were powerless to stop the wholesale plunder of the royal tombs. In the end they gave up. Tidying up disordered burial chambers and ceremonially re-sealing the few remnants left by the thieves was not enough, and if anything at all were to be salvaged for the future life of the royal dead, drastic steps would have to be taken. They assembled the mummies of some 40 of the greatest kings and queens and spirited them out of the valley and over the hills which form its boundaries to a place they had prepared, high in the cliffs over Deir el-Bahari. A cleverly concealed shaft was sunk in the rock 60 metres above ground level. It dropped straight down for nearly 12 metres; from the bottom of the shaft a passage less than a metre high ran in a westerly direction for 7.40 metres then made a right-angled turn to the north. For 60 more metres this passage continued, sometimes wider and sometimes narrower, dropping at one point down a few rough steps and finally opening into an oblong chamber. No attempt was made to beautify the tomb or to conduct rites of fitting richness and dignity for its illustrious occupants. They and the remainder of their funeral goods were huddled pell-mell into the chamber, and left.

This time the priests succeeded. Perhaps the obvious haste and secrecy of this last removal achieved their object, or perhaps the word had gone round that there was nothing of value left to steal; whatever the reason, the mummies remained undisturbed till the operations of modern thieves uncovered their hiding-place and ultimately led the authorities to the spot, ending in the bizarre procession down the Nile to their last resting place in the Cairo Museum.

The practice of tomb-robbing was probably as widespread as, and only a matter of hours less ancient than, that of conducting rich burials.

opposite A box lid wrenched from its hinges and flung into a corner displays a highly unusual combination of courtly splendour and domestic tenderness in the scene it depicts. Made of ivory veneer carved in low relief and coloured, it shows Tutankhamun and his wife in a garden, the queen offering her husband a bouquet of mixed lotus and papyrus flowers. They both wear court dress of pleated linen, elaborate wigs and magnificent collars, but there is a touching air of intimacy in the portrayal of the young couple which could only be associated with the Amarna period. Egyptian Museum, Cairo.

There is evidence that it was already well established in the Old Kingdom era, and that then as later, the necropolis staff were the collaborators of the thieves if they were not actually the perpetrators of the robberies. As time went on collaboration between tomb workers and tomb robbers was developed to a fine art. Respect for the dead was replaced by such a degree of callous cynicism that the officials who performed the burial ceremony seldom left much in the way of easily portable pickings for later thieves, except the amulets and personal jewellery sealed inside the mummy case with the body itself, which could not readily be pilfered in passing. To acquire these they evolved a system which, for ghoulish ingenuity, was worthy of Burke and Hare. They designed a coffin with a false section near the head in the form of a wooden panel painted with the same finish as the rest and held lightly in position by flimsy wooden pegs. A few taps would be sufficient to displace it; the body could be hauled out through the opening and rifled without incurring the labour, noise and danger involved in removing the massive coffin lid to get at its contents.

The process of building a new tomb often endangered the occupants of neighbouring ones, assuming that they had not already been plundered by the necropolis priests when they were first buried. The graves were sometimes so close together that as the labourers hollowed out a chamber they only had to pierce a hole in the wall to gain access to the adjoining tomb. They took care to preserve the plug of rock which, when carefully replaced, adequately hid their mode of entry while keeping it available for further raids. Some burials were obviously carried out in a hurry, or at a time when few resources were available. One of these was Princess Entiu-ny, daughter of the Twenty-first Dynasty ruler Psusennes I (1070–1052 BC). When she died she was not accorded the dignity of a tomb of her own. The officials of Deir el-Bahari merely re-opened the grave of Queen Merytamun who lived in the mid-15th century BC, daughter of Thutmose III and wife of Amenhotep II. As they made their way down the entrance passage they discovered that the Eighteenth Dynasty masons had sunk a deep pit in the floor, so they stopped at this point, bundling the princess's coffin into the passage along with an untidy huddle of grave goods. The later excavators were more conscientious. They laid planks across the pit and crawled over, finally penetrating into the chamber where Merytamun's enormous coffin lay staring upwards in the uncertain light of their torches. Others before them had not been deterred by the pit. The queen's mummy still lay inside, but it had been looted, apparently more than once. The bandages still bore the imprint of the circlet she

The desolate Valley of the Kings on the west bank of the Nile near Thebes was chosen by some of Egypt's greatest rulers to be their burial place – a vain attempt to avoid the attentions of the tomb robbers. The complex of low stone walls in the centre foreground, just in front of the diagonal cutting of the entrance to Rameses VI's tomb, is the site of the tomb of Tutankhamun.

had worn on her head, and the shell of her coffin showed the marks of the gold sheathing torn off by the robbers. Priests who still preserved some sense of decorum and duty had done their best to restore order, repairing and repainting the coffin and re-wrapping the mummy. They recorded their pious act with an inscription found on its breast which read 'Year 19, Month 3 of Akhet, Day 28' or, in contemporary terms, 25 November 1049 BC.

Reburial after a robbery was a common occurrence, but sometimes the whole ceremony had a distinctly farcical element, whether or not the participants were aware of it. Investigating the area around the Great Pyramid at Gizeh in 1924–5, G. A. Reisner came across a rock that seemed to be marked with plaster. Clearing the surface, he found a flight of steps leading down to a tunnel. This ended in a vertical shaft blocked with stone, in the walls of which were niches filled with ritual objects. They finally reached the burial chamber with its white alabaster sarcophagus, the lid of which was sealed and still in position. This was not all. The burial, judging from the accompanying tomb furniture and its proximity to the pyramid of Cheops, belonged to an important personage, but it was some time before they could learn the identity of the occupant. The chamber was rough and unfinished, and there was a general air of haste and muddle which contrasted strangely with magnificent equipment. Inlaid armchairs, chests of jewellery, gold and silver furniture including a splendid canopied bed and a golden palanquin were clearly royal appointments which claimed the excavators' attention at once because of their extreme fragility. The wooden structure of the furniture had disintegrated, leaving only the gold sheathing and

The direct predecessor of Tutankhamun was the heretic pharaoh Akhenaten, shown here on a relief from Tell el Amarna, with his beautiful wife Nefertiti and two of their daughters, receiving the life-giving blessing of the sun-god Aten. The unusual realism of Amarna art stresses the curious physique of the king, with his emaciated arms, hollow face and full, almost feminine hips. Some experts believe that these physical peculiarities suggest that he suffered from a rare disease which may have affected his mind.
Ägyptisches Museum, Berlin.

The problems and pressures involved in clearing the tomb of Tutankhamun included more than the age and fragility of the objects themselves. As soon as the discovery was made public Carter was bedevilled not only by the rough terrain and the lack of good roads or transport, but by the eager presence of hordes of sight-seers, all determined to get a front line view of the century's most spectacular find.

the inlays which had to be collected and re-constructed fragment by fragment using tools no coarser than tweezers and a camel-hair brush.

As they worked through the burial chamber, the investigators' minds frequently turned to the problem of identifying the occupant. A piece of gold inscribed with the name and titles of Sneferu proved a false lead; this pharaoh already had pyramids at Dahshur and Meidum, and the tomb furnishings seemed to indicate a woman. The answer was provided by an inscription on the back of the palanquin. It was the tomb of Hetep-heres, mother of Cheops himself. They deduced, from the signs of hurry and the skimpy workmanship of the chamber, that the contents had been removed from else-where to protect them from robbers and re-buried at the order of the king, close to his own future resting-place. For the whole season they laboured patiently on the contents of the tomb, but always the great white sarcophagus with its intact lid awaited them. Then at last they raised the top, and living eyes peered into the inside for the first time since the 3rd millennium BC. It was empty.

In a moment of supreme anticlimax they stared ruefully at each other, and then the speculations started. Finally they surmised the course of events. Thieves had attacked the queen's original tomb. With little time at their disposal and possibly no means of transport to

remove the bulkier objects they made straight for the most compact and valuable articles which, they must have deduced, would have been those wrapped among the bandages on the royal mummy. There was no time to unroll all the metres of linen swathing the corpse so they lifted it bodily out of the coffin and made off with it. When the priests discovered the theft there must have been a very nasty moment for one of them as they decided who was going to report this sacrilege to the queen's devoted and pious son. Possibly they did not know that the coffin was empty; but it is hard to believe that they had not inspected the most important item in the tomb, or that the thieves left no traces of their operations on the coffin. It is more likely that they simply dare not give an account of this fearful desecration and face the wrath of the pharaoh, who would have held them responsible. So a new tomb was prepared, and the priests and the pharaoh went through the solemn farce of interring the uninhabited coffin with royal honours and filial respect.

But in one case, the most notable in the history of archaeology, the opening of the tomb of Tutankhamun by Howard Carter in 1922, the situation was reversed. This time, the archae-ologists, who expected to find little more than the usual plunderers' rejects, were rewarded by the only royal burial to be preserved almost intact in the Valley of the Kings. It is necessary to qualify the 'intact' description because, con-

below Howard Carter and his Egyptian assistant, working in the cramped and airless space of the burial chamber of Tutankhamun's tomb, examine the set of nested coffins which contained the mummy of the young king. Their instruments, ranging from a formidable mallet to the finest brushes and tweezers, reflect the variety of the problems they might be called upon to tackle in the course of the work.

opposite One of the finest and most fragile treasures from the tomb of Tutankhamun was a wooden chest coated with fine white gesso plaster and painted in brilliant colours. The side panel shows the king in a chariot drawn by plumed horses, his enemies fleeing and falling in disorder before his deadly arrows – a complete fantasy as there is no historical evidence that he ever saw a battle in his short life. Egyptian Museum, Cairo.

trary to the general opinion, the tomb of Tutankhamun did not entirely escape despoliation. Thieves broke into it not once but twice and there can be little doubt that it would have shared the fate of all the others had it not been for the political disturbances at the end of the Eighteenth Dynasty and the grandiose pride of the young king's Twentieth Dynasty successor, Rameses VI, over 100 years later.

The burial, far from being a mere lucky strike, was found as the result of years of preliminary investigation and logical deduction. Its presence was little or no surprise to Carter; it turned up in that out-of-the-way corner of the Valley of the Kings because there was nowhere else it could be. Only the contents came as a surprise; and what informed archaeologist could, in his wildest moments of optimism, have foreseen that dazzling prize?

For more than 100 years before the discovery, one archaeologist after another had been successively turning their backs on the Valley of the Kings with the confident pronouncement that it was now fully investigated and no further burials could be expected there. Certainly, between the ministrations of ancient tomb-robbers and modern investigators, the site had been perhaps more exhaustively probed than

any other, and the incentives were such as to provide every imaginable reason literally to leave no stone unturned. At the beginning of the present century it seemed to virtually everyone that in the Valley of the Kings, as on the plateau at Gizeh, not a king's tomb remained unplundered. Among the few dissenters was Howard Carter, and he had no permission to excavate.

From 1902 until 1914 the vital concession to dig the Valley of the Kings was held by Theodore Davis, who made a number of spectacular discoveries and then, like his predecessors, declared the site to be exhausted and handed on his concession to the eagerly waiting Carter and his enlightened backer and patron the Earl of Carnarvon. Carter had something more concrete than the unformulated curiosity of the early treasure-hunters to motivate his search. Even before he took up the concession he knew what he was looking for and had a fair idea of whereabouts he would find it. The tomb of Tutankhamun was his aim from the start of the excavation.

On the face of it this sounds like an extravagant claim. Tutankhamun was, at that time, little more than a name in the Egyptian king-list whose brief reign occurred almost at the chaotic

end of the Eighteenth Dynasty. He succeeded the strange 'heretic' pharaoh Akhenaten, who challenged the Theban priesthood and, finding that even his own mighty office lacked the power to breach the bastions of religious orthodoxy built up over so many centuries, had taken himself and his followers and family off to found a new city dedicated to the new monotheistic cult of the Aten, the life-giving sun. He had no sons and, according to Egyptian custom, his eldest daughter's husband was his legal successor. The eldest, however, died young, the second was unmarried, and the third became the wife of Tutankhamun (or Tutankhaten, as he was known at the time of the marriage). Who exactly this young man was has been the subject for tomes of scholarly conjecture, but it was sufficient for the Egyptians that he was consort of the late king's eldest surviving daughter, and as such he succeeded to the throne. He and his wife were very young, and the combined influence of the priesthood and their elder relatives soon prevailed upon them to drop Akhenaten's short-lived deviation from the paths of orthodoxy and return to the safe beliefs of their forefathers in Thebes, where Tutankhamun is credited by the inscriptions with a sweeping programme of restoration of order

and harmony at home combined with heroic and (of course) victorious military exploits abroad. Considering that he can scarcely have been more than 18 when he died, it is far more likely that he simply did as he was told, died young and was afforded a hurried and unpretentious tomb in a modest corner of the Valley of the Kings. Modest indeed, for it succeeded in doing what no other royal burial did in almost entirely escaping the notice of the ancient tomb-robbers. But not that of Howard Carter.

Most of the kings buried in the valley were accounted for, chiefly by their stripped and empty graves, but no one seemed to have thought of Tutankhamun, until Davis's excavations unearthed a faience cup bearing the young pharaoh's name. Close by was a small tomb in which were a few objects and an assortment of fragments inscribed with the names of Tutankhamun and his wife and family, and not far away the same excavator had uncovered a rock-cut niche full of sealed jars which later transpired to contain the ritual debris left over from Tutankhamun's funeral. This combined evidence seemed to Carter the strongest indication that, contrary to Davis's opinion, Tutankhamun's grave must be in this area and still undisturbed, though after so many years of non-

page 130 top The decorative plaque of a pectoral, once fitted to a chain or bead necklace, shows Nekhebet, the vulture goddess, who often appears in association with Buto the cobra as symbols of the kingdoms of Upper and Lower Egypt.
Egyptian Museum, Cairo.

page 130 bottom As Carter and his team struggled in the narrow space of the burial chamber of Tutankhamun's tomb, they were puzzled by the difficulty they found in lifting the contents of the great shrine. This was explained when they came to the innermost coffin, which proved to be of solid gold and therefore immensely heavy. The likeness of the king as Osiris, the symbols of his rank crossed on his breast and the cobra and culture of upper and lower Egypt on his brow, have all been shaped in gold to contain the body itself.
Egyptian Museum, Cairo.

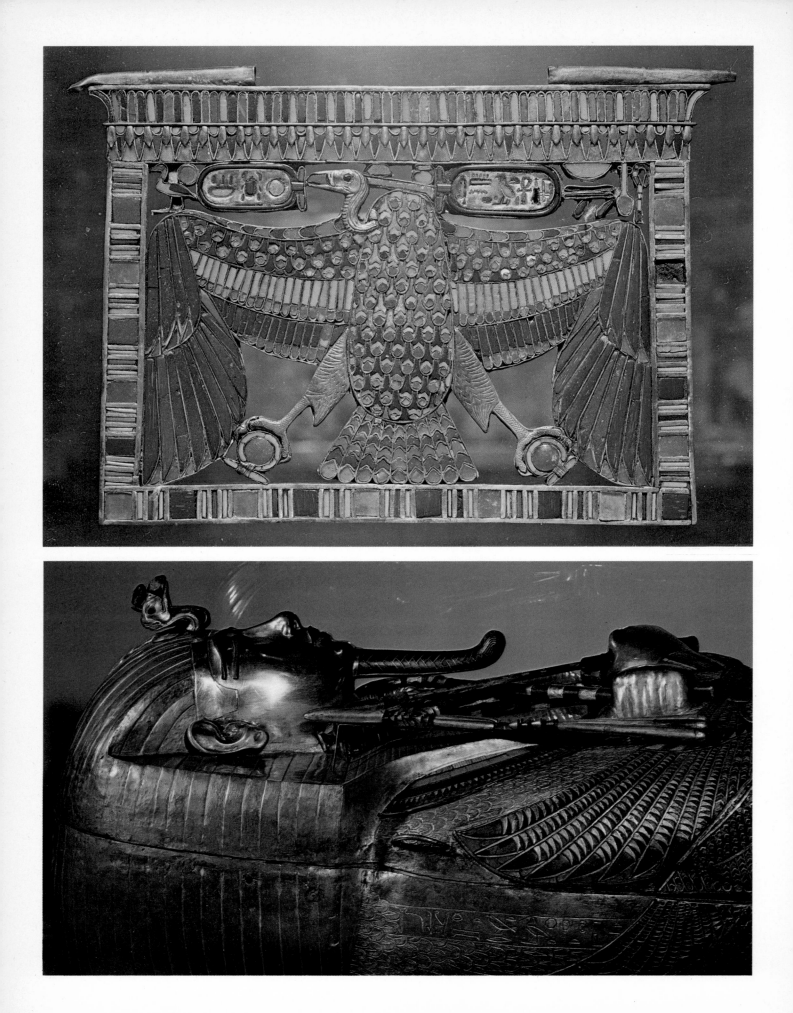

top and bottom left see page 129.   *below* see page 133.

stop rummaging and burrowing the idea might reasonably have been dismissed as impossible.

It was, therefore, with well-founded and justifiably high hopes that Carter at last led his team into the valley to hunt for the tomb of Tutankhamun, only to find several more years of frustration awaiting him. 1914 was not a propitious year to embark on a major undertaking, and the First World War had to run most of its tragic course before he could at last get down to work. In 1917 he was finally able to tackle the project for which he had waited so long and prepared so thoughtfully.

Even though the rough limits of the area to be investigated were suggested by Davis's finds there was still a formidable amount of work to be done. Vast piles of sand and rock, the accumulated debris of former excavators, legal and illegal, lay thick on the ground, and the only way to be sure that the search had missed nothing would be to dig all the way to virgin ground. Steadily and methodically, recording every step with meticulous care, they pushed forwards from the outer edge of the selected area towards the tomb of Rameses VI. This elaborate complex had needed a large labour force to construct it, and the ancient workmen had lived on the site in a series of small huts roughly built near the mouth of the tomb. Carter viewed the remains of these huts with interest. Their undisturbed presence indicated unexcavated ground underneath them, and they were built on a heap of rocks of the type that was often associated with the presence of a tomb.

Once more Carter was delayed. The Rameside tomb was one of the great tourist attractions of the valley, and he could not block access to it with his excavations at the height of the season. He decided that, since these few square metres were the last unexplored ground in the area, he must wait until just before the start of the next season, when he could finish off the dig in a few days without interfering with the movements of the public; there was, in fact, a good deal of debate as to whether there was any point in going on at all. He had so very little to show for several years of the most detailed investigation, and so very small an area remained unexcavated that his colleagues felt it might be wiser to devote the remainder of the concession to other potentially more fruitful districts.

Carter, however, was not convinced. He still believed in the evidence of Davis's finds, and his imagination was still drawn by those temptingly undisturbed huts below the Rameside tomb; he was not prepared to abandon the valley until he had explored the last centimetre of the promising spot. In early November 1922 he set about clearing away the huts, and underneath the very first was revealed the beginning of a flight of steps leading down into the earth

and concealed since before the building of the Rameside tomb. Without question he had found the entrance to a hitherto unknown burial; and when the stairs were cleared, the doorway at their foot proved to bear the seal of Tutankhamun.

Thus far the element of logical deduction; he had studied the facts and deduced from them that the tomb must exist somewhere in this area, and his persistence was fully vindicated. But chance still had a considerable part to play. How could he dare to hope that this tomb alone, of all those in the Valley of the Kings, had escaped plundering? Yet another possibility existed: perhaps it was not a tomb at all—it seemed suspiciously small for the great days of the Eighteenth Dynasty—but a cache of bits and pieces gathered together from a raided burial. At first there seemed all too much reason to believe that ancient robbers had been there before him and that he might find nothing but the fragments they had left behind. The tomb had vanished from sight by the Twentieth Dynasty; but when he had cleared the staircase, in the fill of which were quantities of broken material, some of it dating back as far as the reign of Thothmes III (a bad sign in itself), he saw that the priests of the necropolis had found it necessary to re-plaster and re-seal the doorway, not once but twice.

Despite this discouraging fact, there was still much to be hoped for from the tomb. The priests would hardly have bothered to re-seal it unless something of value had been left, and with this reflection to keep up his spirits as best he might, he dismantled the plaster of the doorway, only to find the passage beyond it blocked from floor to ceiling with rubble. It was clear that a narrow tunnel to the inner doorway of the tomb proper had been driven through this fill, amongst which yet more disquieting evidence was found. More broken pottery, some of it the remains of fine alabaster jars, the waterskins used by the

opposite One of several state chairs retains the forms of earlier folding stools, but is made of ebony with rich inlaying of symbolic religious motifs. Gold, ivory, faience, coloured glass and gem-stones decorate the back and the accompanying footstool, while the broad seat is worked to imitate black and white cow hide. Despite the official return to the Theban religion, the sun-god Aten figures prominently among the symbols.
Egyptian Museum, Cairo.

page 131 Within the third, pure gold, coffin of Tutankhamun lay the young king's body, swathed in many metres of fine linen, loaded with jewellery and amulets and, over its head and shoulders, an exquisite portrait mask of beaten gold. The great folded head-dress was inlaid with strips of blue glass, which also forms the details of the royal insignia and the Osiris beard.
Egyptian Museum, Cairo.

The jewellery which lay closest to the king's body included some superb examples of the goldsmith's craft, most of which had amuletic significance. A pendant in the form of Horus the hawk god is exquisitely inlaid with multi-coloured glass and gems, each piece separately cut with astonishing accuracy to fit its individual cell made of thin strips of gold.
Egyptian Museum, Cairo.

plasterers who had repaired the inner doors, and any number of fragments of loot dropped and trampled in the plunderers' hurried retreat were extracted from the passage-way. Clearly there had been a first robbery after which the priests had filled the passage with rubble to deter further raiders, but had not managed to do so. The tunnel represented a second attempt, obviously successful, to reach the treasure-chambers beyond, and the theory that the tomb was only a cache, the hurried clean-up of perhaps several burials, began to look even more depressingly likely.

Carter's suspense did not last long. In one of the most dramatic moments in the entire history of archaeology he introduced a light through a small opening he had made in the inner doorway beyond the passage, and saw the tumbled mass of golden treasures within. The days that followed passed in a frenzy of demanding but richly rewarded activity. Thieves had indeed broken into the tomb, with its antechamber, annexe, burial chamber and store room all crammed with treasure, but how far they had penetrated could not be ascertained at a glance. Their very footprints still marked the dust on the floor, and the wild chaos of the tomb's interior was a disturbing contrast to the neat arrangement of carefully labelled and sealed containers, each with its contents listed on a docket, which funerary ritual decreed. However, these lists proved that though the king's treasures had been flung about with wild disregard for order and propriety, very little indeed was actually missing.

Self-restraint on a titanic scale must have been needed to work through this fabulous golden dump, much of it incredibly fragile and all of it unique in interest and importance. The bone-dry air of the tomb, undisturbed since some 15 years after the funeral, had preserved even fine wooden furniture and plaited rush sandals (only leather seemed to have succumbed to the passing centuries), but all the organic material had become so brittle and desiccated that it might crumble into dust if so much as an untoward breath of air were to catch it. Beds, chairs and boxes were coated with a layer of fine gesso, lightly modelled and gilded or painted with brilliant artistry, but in many cases the wood had warped or shrunk, dangerously loosening the decoration. Delicately embroidered or finely beaded linen garments were bundled up heedlessly among heavier, sturdier materials. All these objects, and thousands more, had to be studied, recorded and photographed before they were touched, and then treated as far as possible *in situ* to prepare them for transport from the valley to the safety of the Cairo Museum. Even under the most propitious circumstances it would have been demanding

work; in the airless, constricted antechamber of the tomb, knee-deep in frail, priceless treasures, the problems must have seemed almost insuperable. But Carter's patience, skill and ingenuity never faltered.

To add to his difficulties, the world was now swept with an unprecedented epidemic of what might be called pharaoh-fever. Everyone wanted to know about the finds, and as many as possible – far too many for the excavators' comfort – wanted to see for themselves. The world's press and hordes of tourists converged eagerly on the valley. There was no thought now of providing access to the Rameside tomb. No doubt for the first time in his august existence the mighty Rameses had to take a back seat to an insignificant boy scion of the burnt-out Eighteenth Dynasty. Carter's own comments on the behaviour of the general public are tactful and restrained, but there is no mistaking the note of asperity with which he describes the obstructions and aggravations caused by the crowds of sensation-seekers pressing round the tomb.

Through all the team's first seasons of work one great question still remained to be answered. At the back of the antechamber was the sealed door to the burial room itself – with a thieves' hole clearly visible under the hasty repairs carried out by the priests. There was always the possibility that all this magnificence might surround an empty coffin, as the excavators of the tomb of Hetep-heres had found. However, Carter could not afford to rush. The antechamber was methodically cleared before he would consider embarking on the investigation of the inner room. Here they found that conditions were even more confined, for the great golden shrine enclosing the burial almost filled the little room. Their efforts, however, were immeasurably heartened and encouraged by the discovery that once they had penetrated beyond the first of the shrines, evidence of the ancient thieves disappeared. The original seals were unbroken, the funerary garlands and amulets lay untouched where they had been reverently laid during the last rites for the young king, and they knew now that they could confidently expect to find Tutankhamun himself in the innermost coffin. Although Carter's findings to date far outranked any others in importance, an empty coffin would have been a sad note of anticlimax. Luck was on his side, however, and he was spared the ultimate disappointment.

This inspiration was a very necessary incentive as he struggled with the difficulties of investigating the burial chamber. The great golden shrine proved to be only the outer layer of a veritable nest of treasures, all fitted inside each other with only millimetres to spare, some actually stuck together by the dried remains of the funerary libations, and most made of super-

lative workmanship in delicate, horribly perishable materials. No fewer than four shrines of thick, heavy wood coated with gilded gesso came first; then a massive sarcophagus of yellow quartzite with a granite lid, all draped in a spangled linen pall; and within it, the three human-shaped coffins of the king, the outer two of gold-plated wood inlaid with coloured glass and gems and the third (which explained the vast weight with which the excavators had to wrestle) of pure, solid, exquisitely engraved and jewelled gold.

The process of freeing, dismantling and removing all these infinitely precious objects from the cramped little burial chamber was an epic of resourcefulness in itself; but at last the lid of the golden coffin was removed and there lay Tutankhamun, swathed from head to foot in fine linen wrappings, loaded with layer after layer of protective charms and wonderful jewellery, his head covered by a beaten gold mask which portrayed with consummate artistry the touchingly youthful features of the king in the mournful dignity of his guise as Osiris. When the face of the mummy was finally revealed, all the experts who were present testified to the excellence of the likeness.

The unwrapping of the mummy, however, brought Carter's first major disappointment. The wrappings and the body itself were entirely permeated by funerary unguents which had been lavishly poured over each stage of the burial (Carter estimated that at least two bucketsful must have been used). The thick, tarry liquids had solidified and carbonised, not only sticking the coffins, the wrappings and the mummy together but wreaking havoc with any organic material they touched. Only the head and feet of the body had been spared, and even they were somewhat damaged by proximity. However, shrunken and discoloured as it was, Tutankhamun's face still showed a delicacy of feature which testified to his good looks in life, and an unmistakable resemblance to the royal family which indicated a close blood relationship. It was a solemn and emotional moment for the excavators when the daylight fell on the young face for the first time in 33 centuries.

This is, perhaps, an appropriate point to deal with that most persistent and hoary myth, the Curse of the Mummy's Tomb. For some unfathomable reason which probably has more to do with Boris Karloff's script-writers than Tutankhamun, a story emerged soon after the opening of the tomb which perpetuated the notion that when the grave was sealed a terrible curse was pronounced on anyone who dared to disturb its hallowed repose, and that thereafter the members of the excavation team were hounded by death, digrace and misfortune by mysterious and malignant forces. This absurd fantasy may have arisen from the fact that Lord Carnarvon died the year of the opening of the tomb as the result of an infected mosquito bite. So, no doubt, did hundreds of other people who had never so much as heard of Tutankhamun, but – 'The Curse', crowed the occult-minded public dramatically, regardless of the fact that the Earl had suffered from persistent enfeeblement and ill-health ever since a road accident which occurred long before he ever visited Egypt. In his book, Howard Carter waxes angry over the mere suggestion. 'All sane people', he writes, 'should dismiss such inventions with contempt. So far as the living are concerned curses of this nature have no place in Egyptian ritual. On the contrary we are piously desired to express our benevolent wishes for the dead. That a similar spirit of wise charity should be absent in the loose-tongued gossips referred to, strongly suggests that, in some respects, our moral progress is obviously less than kindly people generally believe.'

In retrospect one can only say that the elusive curse, if it ever existed, was singularly ineffective. Howard Carter, the man who deduced the existence of the tomb, located it, stripped it of its treasures and with his own hands broke open the seals to bring the young pharaoh out of his sacred resting place, lived to a ripe age and died full of years and honours in 1939 – a longevity shared by many Egyptologists who devoted their entire lives to despoiling the ancient dead.

It might fairly be claimed that in this case there was no call for curses, for Tutankhamun still lies in his tomb in the Valley of the Kings. When the investigations were complete and science had had its day, sentiment was allowed its turn, and the body was replaced in one of its coffins (not, needless to say, the solid gold one) in the burial chamber. Sentiment, indeed, was never far away, for throughout the excavation evidence had occurred from time to time that something warmer than official piety had been at work in preparing the king's burial place. Someone had remembered the tiny chair he had sat in as a child, several toys and games, a lock of the henna-red hair of Queen Tiy, who may have been his grandmother. Priests and servants would have packed up the slings he had used, but surely only a closer, more personal affection would have recollected that slings are no use to a boy without stones, and gathered a little hoard of smooth round pebbles for him to use. Laid on one of the inner coffins, in touching contrast with the stiff, splendid funerary collars and bouquets, was a tiny wreath of simple flowers. Tutankhamun's burial, modest and even impoverished as it must have been by the standards of his own day and age, was conducted not with curses but with love.

The Dead Sea Scrolls

Of all archaeological materials perhaps the most fragile are organic remains such as leather, flesh and natural fibres. They seldom survive at all, and when they do it is only because of a combination of unusual circumstances. For example, the acids of the Danish peat-bogs 'pickled' Tollund Man in a perfect state of preservation, his garments and head-gear intact and his face still wearing its curiously serene expression although the rope which had strangled him was still in place round his neck. This was an exceptional case, for as a general rule the moist air and soil of Europe rapidly destroys all forms of organic material and the best archaeologists can hope for is the imprint of the carbonised shape of a long-vanished object in the surrounding earth. The best conditions for preserving finds of this type occur in deserts where the total absence of moisture desiccates everything and prevents rotting. Even here, however, natural materials are far from safe, for they may become so dry that they disintegrate at a touch.

It is, therefore, one of the more inexplicable miracles of archaeology that the Dead Sea Scrolls, perhaps the most important hoard of ancient parchment ever known, not only survived nearly 2000 years in an undisturbed hiding place but emerged relatively legible and intact after a good deal of rough handling in a Bedouin encampment, being lugged around Jerusalem and hawked from pillar to post in a battered old suitcase, and being kicked into the corner of an Arab cobbler's shop where they were acquired for use as potential shoe-patching material. No one will ever know how many priceless writings were destroyed during the obscure period of their history immediately after their discovery, but what remained was enough to make sure that biblical studies have been radically changed by it.

In the early 2nd century BC Judaea came within the sphere of influence of the Greek king Antiochus IV Epiphanes, descendant of Alexander the Great's general and successor in Western Asia, Seleucus Nicator. He was not the first to attempt to make the Jews modify their religious beliefs and rites, nor was he the last to fail. He wished to force on them a Hellenised and, as he thought, more rational ritual which would bring them into unity with the rest of the Hellenistic world, as Alexander had dreamed of doing with the whole of his vast empire. Universal harmony is not in itself an ignoble ideal, but it cannot be achieved by suppressing individuality–this has been attempted more than once in history and the results, usually temporary, may be uniform but are never harmonious, as Antiochus learned. The Jews resisted fiercely, and from their numbers sprang a family of brilliant military strategists called the Maccabees under whose leadership Antiochus was driven out, and his unholy practices with him.

This triumph, however, was followed by events which some pious people of Judaea regarded as almost as bad, for the office of High Priest was made over to the Maccabees in gratitude for the victory. To the purist sects this was an outrage and a blasphemy; the Maccabees were not even qualified by birth to hold this highest and most sacred office, and it was sheer pollution for their battle-worn hands to offer sacrifice in the Temple. What is more, calendrical calculation had fallen away from its original purity, and these sects believed that it was now being offered on the wrong day and must therefore be ineffective. In their eyes the Holy City of Jerusalem was hopelessly defiled, and they must withdraw from it if they wished to escape pollution themselves.

Gathering around them a number of like-minded souls, these pious folk left Jerusalem and headed east into the desert until they reached the shores of the Dead Sea. It was not a hospitable spot. To the north the fresh water of the Jordan runs into the Sea where, upon contact with the dense concentration of salts produced by evaporation, it immediately becomes useless to man or beast, and nearby to the south a few brackish fresh-water springs supported a small welcome patch of green vegetation, but Qumran, which they chose for the site of their settlement, enjoyed none of these ad-

opposite For years scholars laboured over the worn and tattered fragments from Qumran trying to reconstruct and transcribe the invaluable texts as far as possible. Even with the up-to-date resources of the modern workshop especially equipped by the Rockefellers and the combined skills of an international team of the world's leading specialists, it was an infinitely demanding task.

vantages. Perhaps they wished to avoid the envy and attention of more worldly people. If so, they could hardly have chosen better. The community built their new home on the site of an earlier structure which had been used as a religious house as early as the 8th century BC but had been abandoned some time before, situated at the edge of the limestone plateau above the Dead Sea, and here they lived, with a few interruptions, until AD 68.

They were not a monastery in the usual sense of the word, for they had their wives and children with them, and endeavoured to be self-perpetuating as well as self-supporting; but there was something monastic about their life-style which was devoted to preserving the total purity of their religion while they awaited the coming of the Messiah who would sweep away the old order with all its wickedness and initiate a new age of which they, the only true believers, would be the elect. In fact, they believed that there would be two Messiahs, one of whom would be a lay leader of the house of David, while the other (who would take precedence in all things over his lay counterpart) would be a priestly Messiah. The group held all property in common, but there was nothing of Communism about their system, for each member was assigned what might be called a spiritual rank and all activities were conducted in order of this rank, the priesthood well to the fore. Membership was neither easy nor automatic, and a long period of probation had to be passed before a neophyte was fully initiated. Once accepted, each member was subject to a daunting array of rules of conduct, transgression of which brought harsh penalties on the head of the sinner.

Despite these prohibitive hardships, a con-siderable following came to Qumran. It is difficult to estimate exact numbers, but the nearby cemetery of over 1000 graves indicates a flourishing society. At any rate, they were far too many for the settlement house which was chiefly designed for administrative, communal and religious activities, and many of them re-paired some 1000 metres away to the marl terraces and limestone cliffs overlooking the Dead Sea. These were honeycombed with caves, some no more than small fissures in the rock, but others big enough for habitation, and here the overflow of the community settled. Those who were not attracted by the troglodyte life set up tents and huts in which they lived, but used the small caves for storage. Others again retired to the green area round the springs (modern Ain Feshkha) where they built a small agricultural centre and settled down to pasture the community's sheep and goats and to cultivate the vegetables and date palms on which their lives largely depended. There are no palm-trees left now and the soil does not look conspicuously fertile, but a Byzantine record mentions a later Christian monastery not far from Qumran which succeeded in establish-ing a vegetable garden at Ain Feshkha, and there is plenty of evidence for the cultivation of dates.

The homes in the cliff-caves and at Ain Feshkha, however, were only the periphery of the community. Its heart was the settlement house at Qumran, and the heart of Qumran was the Law. The preservation of the Law in all its pristine purity was the whole aim of life, and in order to be sure that it was transmitted accur-ately, it had to be written down. An important part of the settlement house was the *scriptorium* or writing room, which was located on an upper

In the interior of the Arch of Titus in the Roman Forum is a relief depicting the aftermath of the Jewish Revolt, which depopulated Jerusalem and led to the dispersal of the Jewish people for many centuries to come. Spoils from the ravaged Temple of Solomon (the ritual seven-branched candle-holder is promi-nent) are carried in procession at Titus's Triumph.

floor to give plenty of light. Along the wall of this long, airy room ran a plaster bench in front of which was a curious structure like a long table of brick covered with smooth plaster. Here the scribes crouched day after day copying in a variety of hands and scripts the books of the Old Testament, the hymns, holy writings and rules of their order, with frequent pauses for ritual ablutions whenever the Sacred Name had to be written. They worked on parchment made from home-produced goat- and sheep-skins and, on at least one occasion, on a long roll of thin sheet copper, dipping their quills in ink wells not dissimilar to the 'unspillable' type used in schools before the rise of the ball point and fountain pen.

For nearly two centuries the sect flourished in their desert refuge, tending their crops and herds, processing their produce and toiling over their scripts, and day and night without a break shifts of the faithful sang hymns of praise and chanted over the rules of the Law while they awaited with painful eagerness the coming of the Messiah. But it was not the Messiah who came to Qumran in AD 68 and put an end to their self-imposed exile; it was Vespasian and the Roman soldiers of the Tenth Legion. Absorbed in their devotions, the community seem not to have noticed (or thought important) the outbreak of the Jewish Revolt, but if they were prepared to ignore the Roman Empire, the Romans were not prepared to ignore them. Perhaps Vespasian thought the buildings at Qumran would make a useful guard-post to command the north of the Dead Sea, or perhaps he simply did not want to leave a potential pocket of resistance behind as he moved south. Whatever is the truth, once he had decided on the fate of the sect only an insignificant minor skirmish was needed to carry out his decision. It was never even mentioned in the Roman histories, which seemed to take more interest in his scientific experiments to check the buoyancy of the Dead Sea by picking out a few non-swimmers, tying them hand and foot and throwing them in to see if they would float. It is pleasant to record in passing that they did.

What happened at Qumran in the end is attested only by a few archaeological remains. There was a little resistance, but not much. Only a few stayed to fight. Some may have gone south to join the tragic heroism of the last stand at Masada, and others were perhaps swept up in the ebb-tide of the Dispersion. Whatever happened to the community, before the end they knew the Romans were coming and most of them fled. They could not take their treasures with them, so they hurriedly hid their sacred writings in the cliff caves where they had lived, some wrapped in linen and stowed carefully in jars, others flung in pell-mell at the last minute

and then, scattering like everyone else in the ancient world before the advance of the legions, they left Qumran for ever.

The Romans kept a small garrison in the remains of the settlement for a few years, but they never found the caves. Then Rome went the way of the other great empires. No one else came to live at Qumran, where the scrolls grew thick with dust as years turned to decades and decades to centuries. In 1947 the country was again in a turmoil for the Mandate was in its last year and Jews throughout the world believed that the Dispersion would soon be over. As always, the desert shores of the Dead Sea were as little affected by these events as any part of the land could be. The area was, if possible, even more barren and desolate than when the Qumran sect had lived there, and now it supported only a few Bedouin whose herds of goats were able to snatch a scanty living among the sun-scorched rocks.

The barren and sun-scorched cliffs pitted with caves provided an ideal hiding-place for the treasures of the Qumran community before they were wiped out by the Romans. The scrolls were rediscovered by pure chance when a Bedouin goat-herd, in pursuit of his errant flock, lighted on a cave in which were several jars containing scrolls wrapped in linen.

Young Muhammad Adh-Dhib of the Ta' amireh tribe had set out in pursuit of a stray goat which had clambered up among the rocks, but when he had scrambled after it for a while he came to the conclusion that shelter from the blazing summer sun was, at that particular moment, a more attractive prospect than any recalcitrant animal. He accordingly tucked himself into a shady corner and listlessly passed the time by dozing and flipping stones at any suitable target that caught his eye. A good mark soon came to his notice—a small roughly circular hole in the rocks, not much more than half a metre in diameter—and his next shot scored a neat bull's eye, straight through the opening. What he heard banished boredom in an instant, for it was not the dull thump of his stone landing on sand or the clatter of an impact on rock, but the smash of breaking pottery. Pulling himself up to the opening, he peered in. The cave was bigger than its entrance indicated, and in the dim interior he made out rows of tall jars, one of which had been struck by his projectile. Thoughts of evil djinn, angry at being wakened from the sleep of centuries, flashing across his mind, he loosed his grip and fled in panic.

When he got back to the camp that evening and told his story to a friend he received scant sympathy. His friend scoffed at tales of djinn and pointed out that the jars might be more likely to contain hidden treasure. Feeling much bolder in this sturdily sceptical company, Muhammad returned to the cave next day, taking his friend with him. They squeezed through the entrance with some difficulty, and eagerly examined the contents of the jars. To their great disappointment they found no ancient gold but only bundles of dusty old rags containing rolls of leather covered with strange marks. Some of the jars, they thought, might usefully be employed in the camp, but the leather was too old and fragile to be any good, so they stuffed it carelessly among their few possessions and temporarily forgot it as they moved on to the next grazing ground.

They only remembered the scrolls when they next visited Bethlehem, where they went from time to time to trade their surplus produce. They usually dealt at one of those all-purpose general stores which are common in small towns throughout the world. This particular example was kept by a Syrian Christian called Kando, and included a cobbler's shop among its numerous amenities. The scrolls were no good to the Bedouin but Kando thought he might be able to find a use for the leather and idly kicked them into a corner on the floor. Some days later he began to have second thoughts. The signs inscribed on the scrolls meant nothing to him but he was sophisticated enough to realise that they might conceivably have some value if he could find anyone who could read them. He accordingly rescued them from the rubbish on the floor and took them to St Mark's Convent in Jerusalem.

From the moment the Metropolitan of the convent recognised the potential value of Kando's offering the story of the scrolls is obscured in a fog of evasions and prevarication. It must be remembered that almost everyone involved in the discovery was acting, wishing to act, or trying to act, illegally. As early as Schliemann's day the archaeological powers had been taught a sharp lesson on the dangers of unauthorised digs. The enterprising German had made off with the so-called Treasure of Priam leaving virtually nothing for the country whence it originated (the treasure was last heard of in Berlin at the end of the Second World War; where is it now?). Ever since that time the excavation, transport and sale of antiquities had been controlled by stringent regulations carrying heavy penalties, all of which were being recklessly contravened as villagers, Bedouins and monks all scrambled for a share of the scroll bonanza. To add to the problem, political hostilities had now reached a point where it was often dangerous to go out at all, especially in the Bethlehem district, because of the danger from snipers.

The scrolls surfaced briefly in 1948, only to disappear after a tantalisingly short contact with the academic world. They had come close to it once before when one of them fell into the hands of a professor of the Hewbrew University, who traced it as far as Bethlehem. Unfortunately this alarmed Kando, who promptly hid some of the fragments in his garden where the comparatively damp soil immediately caused them to decompose beyond repair. Meanwhile the Metropolitan had been attempting for some months to find out the true age, meaning and (of course) price of his windfall, and at this time his search led him to the American School of Oriental Research in Jerusalem. The Deputy Director, Dr J. C. Trever, did not need more than a superficial examination before he understood that he had something of the utmost importance on his hands. It was a copy of the Book of Isaiah, and he was not able to compare it with any other because it was obviously several centuries earlier than the oldest existing text. The responsibility was enormous, and he decided, in those troubled times, that it would be best to maintain a discreet silence about the discovery—whilst privately taking photographs of the scroll and urging the Metropolitan to remove his previous texts to safety out of the country.

In this way some 18 months elapsed between Muhammad's discovery of the cave and the

To the Essene community, Jerusalem had become an
uninhabitable pollution, and they had to withdraw to a
place where they could wait for the coming of their two
expected Messiahs untouched by the impious influence
of the capital, but near enough to be at hand when the
moment came. Their choice fell on a stretch of arid land
by the cliffs overlooking the Dead Sea, where there was
little likelihood that the impurities of the world would
impinge upon their devotions.

The community had a little warning of Vespasian's approach and began by packing their scrolls, neatly wrapped in linen, in tall earthenware jars with lids in preparation for their evacuation. The legions evidently moved faster than they anticipated, for towards the end the inhabitants of Qumran had no time to do more than throw their writings out of sight into the caves.

When the Essene community withdrew from Jerusalem, they established themselves at Qumran on the shores of the Dead Sea, where the remains of their settlement house can still be seen.

publication of news of the find, which American expert Professor Albright now confirmed to be unquestionably ancient and of the greatest possible significance for biblical studies. Once it was out in the open the source of the scrolls became an urgent problem that could be shelved no longer. It had to be found and safeguarded, for obviously there might be more where these came from, and in any case, the accompanying archaeological material must be found and studied, for it might supply valuable evidence on the date and circumstances in which the scrolls were originally deposited. The authorities of the Antiquities Service and the Archaeological Museum made heroic efforts to trace the source – in such dangerous times more than a touch of heroism was called for in those who had business in disputed territory – and before long they came to understand that they were dealing with badly frightened men. Now that the astronomical market value of the scrolls was public knowledge it was more than anyone's life was worth to divulge the secret of their hiding place. Largely by accident Mr Joseph Saad, the Secretary of the Archaeological Museum, learnt that they came from a cave overlooking the west shore of the Dead Sea not far south of the mouth of the Jordan. This was a start, but nothing like enough. The whole area for miles around was pitted with hundreds of caves of every shape and size. It might take years to find the right ones, and in the meantime they knew, the clandestine excavators were hard at work with all their superior knowledge of the area.

Knowledge of the area ... The sight of a member of the Arab Legion standing guard at the Museum put the idea into Mr Saad's head as he returned, discouraged, after another abortive meeting. The troops of the Arab Legion spend most of their lives in conditions very similar to those of the Dead Sea shores. If anyone could spot clues and follow pointers to the

right caves, they could. After a hurried round of the military authorities, a small detachment was sent to the cliffs and in less than three days a phone call from the officer in charge came through: they had found the cave.

At last, on 15 February 1949, a team of fully trained archaeologists were able to start work on the caves. However, their troubles were not over now that they had found the source of the scrolls. Earlier illegal excavators, their minds fixed on the cash value of the writing which was tentatively established at one pound sterling per square centimetre, had attacked the cave with all the delicacy and discrimination of a Florida hurricane, hurling jars, wrappings and associated finds into a heap outside, irrevocably divorced from the archaeological setting which can be so informative. The team calculated that the cave had once held as many as 40 or 50 jars, and if they had all contained scrolls there must be an enormous quantity of priceless script now in the untrained hands of the Bedouin, the black-market dealers or any one of the numerous unknown middlemen who had managed to corner a share in the enterprise.

While the excavators, often working in stifling heat, sifted the dust in the cave through their fingers in pursuit of the smallest remaining shreds of inscribed leather, the Antiquities Service was making moves to contact the illegal diggers in the hope of retrieving any fragments already in their possession. The first step was to discover the name of the Bethlehem dealer who seemed to be so deeply involved, and this took a prolonged period of alternative bribery and threats. When they finally extracted the information they next had to undertake a horribly dangerous journey through embattled territory to talk to Kando. Several preliminary discussions followed in which Mr Saad sought to gain Kando's confidence and get him to believe that he would suffer no official reprisals and that he would be given a fair price for his fragments. This had to be done without alarming the wily Syrian, or there was more than a chance that he and his hoard would vanish for ever, but after a few meetings he agreed to do a deal. Mr Saad was to meet him in Jericho, bringing along an 'international financier' (actually an assistant of the Antiquities Service) who was interested in buying the scrolls.

The journey to Jericho was bad enough, but on reaching the town they found the rendezvous designated by Kando bristling with sinister-looking thugs who had been recruited to guard the dealer's interests and, if necessary, to secure his retreat. There were many moments of suspense and drama connected with the re-covery of the Dead Sea Scrolls, but none can have been more alarming than walking through this murderous crew with £1000 in cash in their

Simon bar Kochba, who led the Jewish Revolt which was started by Caligula's desecration of the Temple in Jerusalem and ended in the final desperate heroism of Masada, wrote a letter to the Dead Sea community. A battered fragment of the papyrus still survives among the records from the caves.

Bible studies have always been hampered by the fact that the existing texts are copies many times removed from the originals, and inevitably incorporate a number of errors. The Dead Sea Scrolls include several books or fragments of books from the Old Testament which are several centuries earlier than the oldest previously known version. This fragment, from the Book of Exodus, reads:
1. who spoke to Pharaoh, King of Egypt, to bring out the children
2. from Egypt. They are Moses and Aaron. And it happened on the day when spoke
3. to Moses in the land of Egypt
4. Jehovah to Moses, saying, I am Jehovah. Speak to Pharaoh, King of Egypt.
5. which I say unto thee. And Moses said before Jehovah
6. of uncircumcised lips, so how will Pharaoh listen to me? And said
7. to Moses, see, I have made thee a God to Pharaoh; and Aaron thy brother shall be

pockets. It was a great relief when the deal was concluded by exchanging the wad of notes for a heap of dusty pieces of inscribed leather. Kando had been a slippery character to pin down, but once his confidence was gained he was a good confederate. He not only brought more pieces of scrolls to Jerusalem but established contact between the Antiquities Service and the Ta'amireh Bedouins who had found the first cave, and whose unrivalled knowledge of the Qumran cliffs made them useful allies when they were disposed to co-operate.

Even with the whole of the discovery now a matter of public record and an official team busy among the caves, it was still a race with the clandestine looters. Sometimes a tell-tale column of dust rising from the cliff-face in the stagnant air indicated where they were at work, but they had usually vanished by the time the official party reached the spot. Realising that they might be losing important finds which would either vanish for ever or have to be bought back with desperately scanty government funds, the authorities organised a combined operation by the American and French Schools in addition to all the personnel of their own that they could muster. They carried out a complete investigation of the whole cliff nearly as far as Ain Feshkha, searching more than 200 caves in detail. They found more fragments of scroll jars, lamps, coins, cooking and eating vessels, the wooden poles for tents, date-stones and dried dates, scraps of fabric and other plentiful signs that the caves had served as habitations.

For years to come fragments were to come pouring in, from sources both legal and illegal, and it was time to set to work on the gargantuan task of reconstructing, editing, translating and publishing the writings. The enterprise was so great in scope and importance that it was clearly beyond the resources of any one nation, and in the end eight scholars from America, Britain, France, Germany and Poland assembled in Jerusalem, to work in a new institution financed by Mr John D. Rockefeller for the purpose.

First the fragments had to be prepared for study. All of them were thick with dust (luckily the ancient ink was of such good quality that it was not damaged by fairly energetic brushing), and some were so brittle that they could not be smoothed out until they had been treated in a humidifier—a matter of delicate timing, for too much moisture could cause the leather to decompose into a blob of glue. Others were so badly discoloured that the writing was illegible until the team found that the characters were clearly visible if photographed on infra-red film. Others again were ingrained with marl dust that could not be brushed off, and they had to be given a light coat of oil which rendered the marl transparent. The fragments were then laid between sheets of glass on trestle tables for the attention of the scholars in the 'Scrollery', as the chief work room came to be known.

The work could perhaps be most easily envisaged as tackling the biggest jigsaw puzzle in the world: except that in this case there was an unspecified number of puzzles mixed up together with a lot of pieces either defaced or missing altogether. With jigsaw puzzles, too, at least one has the advantage of pieces which fit cleanly together, but the scroll fragments were often so worn and crumbled at the edges that a clean join was seldom possible. The best clue came from the content of the text or the handwriting of the scribe, although the latter might alter as his pen grew worn and in some cases the scroll might be taken over by a different hand altogether. To add to these difficulties, some of the texts were written in an ancient code which had to be cracked before the meaning could be ascertained, or in several ancient scripts and languages.

The copper scroll presented an entirely different problem. It was tightly rolled and crusted with oxidisation and the metal, which

was so thin that the indentations formed by the lettering sometimes showed through, was far too brittle to unwind. Dr John Allegro, one of the team, thought that he knew where the answer was to be found. He applied to the head of Manchester College of Technology and described the difficulty. The college metallurgists were undismayed. Having decided that it would be impossible to preserve the original form of the scroll, they designed an apparatus for cutting it into strips. Most saw blades would have been too coarse for such work but this one was so thin, so delicately balanced and so easily controlled by the operator that it could penetrate one layer at a time when the metal had first been strengthened by applying a coat of epoxy resin. The cutting began. As strip after strip was freed Dr Allegro cleaned them with nylon brush-heads mounted in a dentist's drill, and found that the writing was, on the whole, remarkably legible. It was a record of the Qumran community's treasures which were buried in the area when the Romans were advancing. The only drawback to this exciting discovery is that so far no trace of the treasure has been found; but at least the information is permanently preserved in the scroll.

Considering the complications, it was an amazingly short time before the publications of the scrolls began to appear. The texts consisted chiefly of Old Testament books, (e.g. Isaiah, Samuel and Ecclesiastes), hymns, commentaries, and records of the community's rules and constitution. The importance of these documents for Bible studies was obvious from the beginning. It must be remembered that the Bible as we have it today is the end product of centuries of copying, recopying, editing, translating, correcting and reconstructing, and though stringent precautions were taken at every stage to prevent the introduction of errors and inaccuracies it was inevitable that a number should creep in and that the various versions should increasingly diverge. For this reason, there was immense excitement at the discovery of a manuscript text which pre-dated any known source by several centuries. It shed unprecedented light on the different versions of the Bible, their sources and their comparative accuracy. Of equal importance were the sect's own documents, the only surviving texts setting out the Messianic beliefs of a Jewish community living not far from Jerusalem during the lifetime of Christ.

These scrolls, like the books of the Law and the rules of the group, would have been much more obscure without the support of the archaeological excavations of the caves, the settlement house and the agricultural establishment in the Qumran district. The ancient scholars were prone to express themselves in

The Qumran community soon became too numerous for the settlement house and many of its members elected to live in the caves which honeycombed the cliff face. Here, too, they hid the precious scrolls containing their written records and laws at the approach of Vespasian's legions, and here the scrolls remained undiscovered until the 20th century, their rediscovery coinciding uncannily with the return of the Jewish people to Palestine.

allusions and symbols; for instance, when they spoke of the 'Kittim' (Cypriotes) they meant any people of great military power—in this case, the Romans; 'Damascus' meant a place of exile from Jerusalem, i.e. Qumran, and so on. The excavations clarified many of these obscurities, particularly those concerning the daily life of the sect. They also refuted the inevitable claims that the scrolls were not ancient, the deposit was made in recent years and even that the whole thing was a hoax, and illuminated the Qumran community in a way which the high-minded and spiritual language of the scrolls could never do.

Most of the material connected with the study and excavation of the scrolls remained in the institution built by Mr Rockefeller's grant until after the Six-Day War. It was then transferred to the Israel Museum, where a special complex was built to house it. In the middle of the Shrine of the Book is the great Isaiah scroll, while the others are in display cases round the walls of the rotunda. Ever since their discovery Bible studies have profited immeasurably from the information they provide, and indeed, it would be no exaggeration to claim that the discipline will never be the same again. Archaeology and scholarship can seldom have had such enormous benefits conferred upon them by a run-away goat.

After the Six Day War the Dead Sea Scrolls were taken to the Israel Museum in Jerusalem, where a special building, the Shrine of the Book, was erected to house them. It is an impressive rotunda, in the centre of which the great Isaiah scroll, earliest and most complete text of this book, stands alone on a tall podium. Round the walls are individually constructed display cases for other scrolls and the accompanying material.

Fakes, frauds and forgeries

The collecting instinct is and always has been strong in the human race. This tends to divide those whom it afflicts into two categories: people who collect objects, and people who collect the money of people who collect objects. The vast majority of both dealers and collectors pursue their interests in a perfectly legal and honest manner, but there are others in whom the passion is so strong that they will indulge in any kind of skulduggery to gratify it. Among the most collectable items are the artifacts of the ancient world. The supply is limited and confined largely to official bodies, strictly controlled by laws regulating their export, sale and excavation, and this leaves very little for the private collector who is therefore often ready to pay very high prices. However, where the demand is so great and the rewards so high there are always plenty of ingenious and unscrupulous operators ready to supply it, and this is where the forger comes into his own. Their work ranges from clumsy frauds which ought not to fool the average well-informed 10-year-old (although there are still tourists gullible enough to respond to the sidling figure with his furtive 'Psst! Want to buy some antiquities?', who still haunts some of the sites), to masterly pastiches which have convinced leading experts at the great museums and caused indiscribable embarrassment when the truth finally came out.

The business of forgery is probably as old as the collecting instinct itself, but its earliest traceable manifestations occur in the Roman empire. The city of Rome might have been the centre of the world to its citizens, but Athens still possessed a certain cachet which caused some leading families to send their sons to 'university' there for a final intellectual and cultural polishing, and gave them a taste for decorating their villas and town houses with any works of Greek art and architectural decoration they could acquire. If they could not get originals a Greek craftsman would be only too willing to make copies or to carve pieces in the archaic manner for them. These pieces now have considerable value in their own right, for many of them preserve some idea of a lost original by a Greek master-sculptor, and in any case they are authentic works of ancient art. Indeed, it is possible that in some cases a 'forgery' may be of greater value than an original. What museum would hesitate given a choice between a portrait bust by an undistinguished Roman hack stone-cutter and a genuine Michelangelo 'forged' in the Roman style?

In fact, the great Renaissance sculptor and his contemporaries regarded the production of imitation ancient pieces as a perfectly respectable pursuit, and a considerable school grew up of artists making small bronzes and other collectors' items in the antique style; but the dividing line can easily grow blurred between bronze or stone treated with an antique finish for aesthetic reasons and one which is specifically intended to deceive the buyer. Deceit must also have been encouraged by the common practice of 'restoring, repairing and improving' ancient works. A newly excavated statue is seldom in mint condition–it would be highly suspicious if it were–and from the Renaissance to the early 19th century even the greatest artists were prepared to turn their hands to tidying up the damage of centuries, which often included recutting so drastic that the end product was scarcely recognisable. For instance, Cellini supplied the twin babies Romulus and Remus to 'complete' the Capitoline Wolf, and these exuberantly Mannerist cherubs assort very oddly with the stark late Etruscan animal. Restorers' activities were not confined to missing arms or broken noses, and sometimes included radical rethinking of the carving to make it conform to fashionable notions of what the ancient sculptor ought to have designed. This attitude was particularly prevalent in the Neo-classical era, and Thorwaldsen's curiously characterless reconstructions of the Aegina sculptures are a lamentable example of the damage that could be done. Fortunately some artists seem to have known better. When Lord Elgin bought the Parthenon marbles his first thought was to have them 'retouched' and he approached Canova with a request to carry out the work. This dis-

opposite The word 'forgery' means the making of a fraudulent imitation for financial gain, and as such is punishable by law. But copying work of an earlier date is a tradition almost as old as art itself: to the Romans, and later to the artists of the Renaissance, it was a perfectly legitimate practice. The Romans were so avid for Greek works of art that they were quite prepared to pay an artist to make copies if originals were not available, and many of these, such as this Roman copy of the Cnidian Aphrodite by Praxiteles, are masterpieces in their own right. Vatican Museums.

criminating sculptor replied emphatically that 'it would be sacrilege in him, or any man, to presume to touch them with a chisel'. The world owes an eternal debt of gratitude to Canova.

With so fine a distinction between honest copies, repairs and reproductions and pieces made with the deliberate intention to deceive, with very little in the way of genuine scholarship to discriminate between the two, and with no scientific laboratory tests available to establish authenticity, the traffic in forgeries must have flourished almost unchecked for centuries. It was only in the 19th century, with the founding of most of the great national museums, that the position of the forger began to change. In one respect his rewards and incentives were higher than ever, for from the Industrial Revolution onwards there were far more people with enough money to indulge a taste for collecting. In another way the forger's job was harder; those who cheated a state museum were cheating the state, and the earlier unspoken *caveat emptor* clause did not apply. He no longer had to deceive an unsuspecting and often ill-informed amateur but a panel of the most distinguished experts. It says much for the skill and ingenuity of the forgers that they sometimes succeeded.

There are innumerable variations, but the majority of forgeries fall into two classes; those where a genuine but unremarkable original has been reworked in some way to enhance its value and importance (e.g. by adding a signature or inscription to suggest historical authorship or significance), and those where the forger has such an instinct for style that he is able to start from scratch and produce entirely contemporary pieces in the ancient style. The latter category comprises most of what might be termed the aristocrats of forgery and is by far the more difficult and demanding of the two approaches. The forger not only has to reproduce all the visual characteristics of the style he is counterfeiting without introducing mistakes or anachronisms, he must also understand ancient materials, tools and techniques, as he cannot hope to succeed if he deviates from the originals in any of these respects. If in addition to these considerations he works in precious metals, his outlay will be large and he will need to be very sure of success before embarking on such a costly venture.

No one can name the most successful forgers, since they are by definition the ones whose products still repose undetected in the great museums and galleries. They are very few in number, but there can be little doubt that they exist. However, there are others whose copious output escaped detection for long enough to class them among the outstanding practitioners of forgery, and one of the greatest of these was the Odessa goldsmith, Israel Ruchomovsky. This ambitious craftsman was not a copyist, nor did he elect to work on pieces from an artistically naive and undistinguished period. He was prepared to tackle the most difficult enterprise in the forger's repertoire: the production of a forged masterpiece in the best style of a highly refined and sophisticated era which might have come from the hand of a leading Hellenistic goldsmith of the 2nd century BC. The preparations were meticulous. First came the documentary evidence to create the right climate for the 'discovery'. It became known that in the 2nd century BC the citizens of a Greek colony at the junction of the Dneiper and Bug rivers made an offering of a fine golden crown to the Scythian king Saitaphernes, whose goodwill and protection they hoped to secure.

Early in 1896 the crown – a three-tiered

Renaissance sculptors frequently made objects in the 'antique' style for sale, and just as frequently 'restored and improved' ancient works of art to conform to contemporary style and taste. The well-known Etruscan bronze of the she-wolf dates from the 5th century BC; the twin babies representing Romulus and Remus were supplied by Benvenuto Cellini in 1500. Such a practice would undoubtedly be regarded as sacrilege today. Museo Capitolino, Rome.

conical cap resembling the papal tiara – appeared in Vienna in the possession of a Romanian dealer named Hochman. It contained nearly half a kilo of gold, and it was a superb piece of workmanship. Two bands of relief work showed episodes from the *Iliad* and scenes from Scythian life, separated by zones of decorative motifs and a Greek inscription reading 'The Senate and people of Olbia to the great invincible Saitaphernes.' The top of the cap was formed of exquisitely executed pierced openwork floral scrolls. Ruchomovsky had done his work well. He had modelled every detail on originals of the correct date, but in every case he had modified the pose and arrangement so that no exact replica could be easily identified. There was only one serious error in the piece, and it was this which put the Viennese experts on their guard. He had not needed to age the metal artificially as gold does not alter with time, but a certain amount of battering would have given it a more convincing appearance. Either he could not bring himself to spoil his masterly handiwork or he did not want to risk reducing its value by damaging any important part of it, so he confined himself to bulging and buckling the background, well clear of the figure work.

The price was high – 100,000 *kronen* – and the Imperial Museum finally decided that they could not risk such a sum on a piece which, however spectacular, was in a suspiciously perfect state of preservation, and which was being offered by a dealer of dubious reputation. Hochman realised that he needed collaborators who enjoyed a certain degree of confidence in the world of art dealing, and was able to secure the help of two Viennese who were not yet known as shady operators. They took the tiara

to Paris and offered it to the Louvre. Chance was on their side, for Baron de Rothschild also saw the crown and expressed his intention of snapping it up if the Louvre did not want it. This meant that the Museum had to clinch the deal in a hurry, without too much time for study and second thoughts. They accepted, and on 1 April 1896 the crown was placed on display in the Louvre while the dealers made off with 200,000 francs.

It did not occupy its honoured position unchallenged for long. Before a year was out two great German experts, Professors von Stern and Furtwängler, had appeared in print roundly condemning the piece as a modern forgery. There were, however, just as many scholars ready to come down on the other side and support its claims to authenticity. How the academic wrangling might have ended will never be known, for the matter was finally settled by the villains themselves falling out. Apparently the share-out of the loot had not been made according to their prior agreement, and Hochman sued

A heavily restored figure from the façade of the Temple of Aphaia, Aegina. By the mid-19th century, archaeological work had been begun on the temple itself, but unfortunately several of the carvings had already been removed to the studio of the sculptor Thorwaldsen, who altered them almost beyond recognition. Artists of the Neo-classical era, like those of the Renaissance, tended to radical rethinkings of ancient works in the name of 'restoration'. Staatliche Glyptothek, Munich.

his two confederates, who defended themselves by the extraordinary expedient of confessing the fraud. By this time a suspicious Russian collector was also hot on Hochman's trail and his activities led him to Ruchomovsky's workshop, where he found patterns and trial pieces unmistakably related to the tiara and several objects he had bought himself from the same source. Curiously enough, these ominous revelations did not seem to disturb the Louvre; but after all, they had 200,000 francs worth of vested interest in believing the piece to be authentic.

In 1903 a Montmartre painter created an uproar in the press by claiming that he had made the tiara. This was too much for Ruchomovsky's pride as a craftsman, and soon afterwards a letter appeared in *Le Matin* from a friend of the goldsmith's attributing the crown to its real creator. In the ensuing sensation funds were raised to bring the Russian to Paris, but even face to face with Ruchomosky the authorities were still bent on proving that he and not their fabulously expensive treasure was a fake. The Russian, stung to anger by their disbelief, produced the only undisputable refutation of their charges. Sending for equipment and metal he set to work and before the appalled and increasingly despairing eyes of the experts, he made the beginnings of another crown at least as convincing as the first. The tiara of Saitaphernes is now locked in the vaults of the Louvre and only displayed at exhibitions of forgeries.

Once the truth was known the experts were all quick to point out a large number of discrepencies and inadequacies in the tiara and the other pieces from the same source. It is strange how these had remained so obstinately invisible for the preceding seven years.

Ruchomovsky, like most forgers, had a single speciality. He always worked in the same material, reproducing works from the same date and culture. If men like him are the aristocrats of forgery, the Italian Alceo Dossena must be called the king, for he was a phenomenon fortunately unique in the annals of this practice; he possessed an astounding ability to produce works of art in almost any material and style, from archaic Greek to high Renaissance and Baroque, without copying any identifiable original and with such fidelity to the spirit of the age he was counterfeiting that his sculpture withstood the scrutiny of many of the most knowledgeable experts. It is fashionable nowadays to decry Dossena's work as inept and unconvincing and to wonder how he got away with it; but one can only say that if he succeeded in fooling most of the people most of the time for 10 years, his forgeries cannot have been entirely without merit.

He embarked on his astonishing career almost accidentally during the First World War.

Trained as a stone-mason and carver, he was on leave from the army in Rome one Christmas and, wanting to raise money for Christmas presents, he sold a little stone Madonna in the medieval style which he had made in his spare time. He made no attempt to disguise its contemporary origin, but Fasoli, the dealer who bought it, was deeply impressed by its sensitive evocation of the Middle Ages. Given a convincing ageing treatment, such pieces would have no difficulty in passing for genuine; in fact, even without any artificial patina he managed to find an unsuspecting purchaser who took the Madonna for a price many times higher than he had paid Dossena.

Fasoli was unable to make any substantial use of his remarkable discovery until after the war was over. He then installed the sculptor in a studio near the Piazza di Spagna, took into partnership another unscrupulous dealer named Palesi and set out on 10 years of wholesale deception in the field of art and antiquities.

Dossena himself wore his gifts uncommonly lightly. If he had money enough for a few drinks and nights out with the girls and time enough to amuse himself in idleness between commissions, that was all he wanted. He always claimed that he never deceived anyone. His agents would come to him with an order for an 'imitation' piece in the Etruscan, medieval or Renaissance style as the case may be, and this he duly supplied. Whatever the dealers might claim for it afterwards was none of his business. He worked and was paid as a producer of sculptural pastiches. It is hard to believe that he was really so naive, or so ignorant of the fate of pieces which were making artistic headlines throughout the world, but no complicity on his part could actually be proved. The dealers were more ambitious. In the post-war years, they knew, a number of states, municipalities and individuals who had suffered severe financial hardships were obliged to put their collections on to the market. There could not be a more propitious time for the appearance and sale of previously unknown masterpieces in considerable quantities. All they had to do was find a client and Dossena would do the rest.

Once a forgery was launched it passed from hand to hand, collecting certificates of authenticity from various experts on its way, often to wind up in leading American galleries and museums which paid a total of millions of dollars for Dossena's fakes. The dealers' confidence and daring increased as one piece after another was accepted and prices soared to astronomic heights. In the end they overdid it. The art world inevitably became a little suspicious of so many masterpieces. The works themselves were becoming too much of a good thing. A battered torso, a fragmentary terra-cotta, even an occasional stone or bronze in good condition were acceptable, if they were rare, but after he had successfully fabricated a 'medieval' Italian tomb with inscriptions, escutcheons and carvings, Dossena's agents set their sights still higher. He planned a 16th-century triumphal arch to be incorporated into a provincial building of a suitable age (explaining its previously unrecorded presence might have proved quite a problem), an early Renaissance shrine complete with saints and a Madonna figure to be attributed to no less an artist than Donatello, and a whole Greek temple pediment carved with a battle between gods and giants. This was undoubtedly going too far, and it could only have been a matter of time before the fraud was exposed, but in fact it was Dossena himself who put an end to it.

He had made a good living over these years, but had frittered away all his money as it came, and in 1928, when his wife fell ill and died, he had nothing left to meet the expenses of the funeral. He went to Fasoli and asked for an

One of the most brilliant forgeries of all time was Tiara of Saitaphernes, made by the Russian goldsmith Ruchomovsky, and displayed in the Louvre in 1896 (it is now kept in the vaults). This is not a copy of an existing work, but an 'original', made in the style of a Hellenistic goldsmith of the 2nd century BC; Ruchomovsky also forged documentary evidence to back up what he claimed as his find.

This 'Roman bronze' figure at the British Museum was shown to be a forgery when analysed – it was made of pure zinc.

advance, claiming with some justice that his share of the takings had never reflected the huge prices obtained for his work. In a moment of monumental stupidity and maladroitness Fasoli refused, and Dossena, perhaps believing that his reputation was now so firmly established that it could survive any revelations, hired a lawyer, called in the press and told the whole story. The resulting consternation can readily be imagined. It was not just a matter of the vast sums of cash which had changed hands; many dealers whose entire prospects depended on their unblemished reputations for judgment and probity had more than money to lose, and they fought desperately to prove that Dossena's claims were those of a disgruntled megalomaniac trying to climb to fame and fortune by asserting authorship of so many acknowledged masterpieces. Dossena answered these charges in the same way as Ruchomovsky had done. In the presence of witnesses, including a film crew and a movie camera, he blithely constructed a terracotta archaic Greek goddess, working so quickly and with such assurance, without the aid of models, sketches or studies of originals, that his claim was proved beyond a doubt.

Forty-five works in major collections were subsequently ascribed to him, and there may be others which remain undetected, although modern scientific tests now make some forms of deception almost impossible. Dossena's

This piece, bought in 1923 by the Metropolitan Museum of Art, New York, as a Greek work of the early 5th century BC, was found to be a fake in 1967.

hoax was such a *tour de force* of sustained brilliance that it is sad to record that after his revelations no one would buy his work at all, not even as curios, and he died in the poor-house in 1937. There was, however, an ironic postscript to his remarkable career. In the last year of his life the old man made a Diana the Huntress in the Etruscan style. It was openly acknowleged as his own work and sold without any attempt at fraud for $125, the normal price for a contemporary *objet d'art* of this nature. After its purchase the Diana vanished from the records, but in 1952 the City Art Museum of St Louis paid $56,000 for an Etruscan Diana which many experts now believe to be Dossena's last work.

Etruscan sculpture has always been a favourite with the forgers of antiquities. Lacking the artistic sophistication and intellectual refinement of classical Greek work, it has many qualities of strongly characteristic stylisation which are easy to counterfeit and which make it instantly recognisable. These works are eagerly sought by collectors, and the existence of vast numbers of unexplored tombs makes the frequent appearance of unexplained pieces a perfectly credible occurrence. The British Museum, doyen of the great classical collections, has not been without errors of judgment over Etruscan purchases. In 1860 the remains of two

154

genuine Etruscan sarcophagi were found at Cerveteri. They were shattered into fragments, and a repairer of outstanding skill was sought for the task of reconstructing them. Finally the Pinelli family were recruited. Their work was a triumphant success, and one of the reconstructed sarcophagi is now to be seen in the Villa Giulia museum in Rome. Unfortunately this achievement went to the Pinellis' heads. If they could repair a sarcophagus so convincingly, why should they not repeat the performance, but using home-made fragments? The result was the Castellani Sarcophagus, pride of the British Museum's Etruscan collection until it was exposed as a fraud in the 1930s.

As time passed a new family took the Pinellis' place in the field of Etruscan fakes. The Riccardis had taken to forgery in the same way, moving from legitimate repair work to the creation of sham artifacts, starting with maiolica and progressing to more ambitious Etruscan pieces. They began discreetly with small, comparatively undistinguished terracotta plaques. These made a comfortable profit and at the same time established the existence of a mythical source in the neighbourhood of Orvieto, which was already well known as an Etruscan centre. These modest pieces were produced at intervals until 1912 when Pio Riccardi, the head of the family, died. The business was continued by his enterprising son Riccardo with two cousins. They had bigger ideas than the older generation, and embarked at once on a series of large figures.

Their first attempt was a terracotta warrior well over two metres high, which was bought by the Metropolitan Museum in New York. There were several unusual features about the style of this elongated figure, but these were ascribed by the museum to the idiosyncrasies of a provincial school. Next came a crate of fragments which, when reassembled, formed a colossal head so large that Miss (later Professor) Gisela Richter of the museum's classical department calculated the original height of the complete figure as more than seven metres. Since the ancient Roman writer Pliny recorded that the Etruscans habitually made and fired their terracottas in a single piece, the head gave rise to a tremendous flurry of admiring speculation about the enormous kiln and the formidable technical mastery which must have been needed to cope with it.

Greatly encouraged by these successes, the Riccardis set about their greatest effort to date. It was a huge striding war-god with threateningly upraised arm, wearing a cuirass and a mighty plumed helmet, of painted terracotta. They based their design on a photograph of a tiny bronze in Berlin, which they planned to reproduce with appropriate variations on a vast scale. They constructed the statue in a house in Orvieto, modelling solid legs surmounted by a hollow body built up of coils of clay carefully smoothed on either side. The head and arms were made separately and attached with pegs which they later removed. It was no mean feat to make a figure of this size and weight in moist clay without any internal supports, and working as they did in confined space surrounded with scaffolding it is not surprising that the finished piece was somewhat oddly proportioned, with a stumpy torso and one over-long arm.

Having managed to prevent it from collapsing under its own weight during construction, they were faced with the problem of firing. The figure was 2.70 metres high, and there was no question of reproducing one of the giant Etruscan kilns, so they allowed their clay to dry and then deliberately smashed it. The resulting pieces were baked separately and where uneven shrinkage spoiled the fit, the edges were chipped and ground away. Just before the completion of the figure Riccardo Riccardi, the leading spirit of the enterprise, was killed in a riding accident, and no further figures on this scale were attempted, but the terracotta war-god's story was only just beginning.

After coaxing the Metropolitan's Rome agent with glimpses of fragments and stories of a secret dig near Orvieto, the gang of forgers and

Etruscan sculpture, relatively simple and unsophisticated, has always been a favourite with forgers. This statue of Mars, in the style of Etruscan work of the 5th century BC, deceived the experts at the Metropolitan Museum of Art, New York, who acquired it in 1921.

the dealers who acted as their middlemen persuaded the museum to buy the piece in 1921 for an astounding $40,000. The Metropolitan now owned all three of the major Riccardi fakes and had invested a vast total sum, but they were not entirely happy about their purchase. There was too much prevarication about the source of the statues (whenever the agent asked to see the actual dig he was always put off with excuses), too many minor stylistic oddities, and perhaps the three together were just too good to be true. At any rate, they were not finally put on public display until 1931, and even then the museum did not venture on a definitive publication of its spectacular acquisition until 1937.

There were plenty of scholars who disagreed with New York's estimate of the terracotta Mars, and stated their opinions in the press and journals, but the outbreak of the Second World War gave everyone more serious matters to think about and the problem was shelved until the 1950s. Then the objections began again, at first to be conclusively refuted by the museum. The statue's varnish was said to be artificially aged – but it was not varnished. The clay frit contained modern glass – disproved by analysis

in the museum's laboratories. The paint was a modern pigment – again disproved by chemical analysis. Still, too many questions were being asked for the comfort of the authorities and when they heard that a certain Italian was claiming acquaintance with the makers of all three pieces, they decided it was time for a definitive investigation.

In a sustained piece of brilliant research based on the ideas of a German scholar named Schumann, the administrative head of the museum succeeded in unravelling the technical process by which the Greeks and Etruscans produced their distinctive red and black pottery in a single firing. He discovered that iron-rich clay turns red if fired in an atmosphere with plenty of fresh air but goes black if starved of oxygen by putting damp wood into the kiln. The pottery, he found, was decorated with a slip made of the finest particles of the clay and then fired in an airy kiln where it turned red all over. When this process was complete he added his smoke-producing material which extracted all the oxygen from the surface of the pot, turning it black. When fresh air was readmitted the coarser parts of the pot re-absorbed oxygen and

turned back to red, but the finer fabric of the slip had fused and could not absorb further elements so that it remained glossy black.

Meanwhile other museum experts were conducting wide enquiries into ancient technique and style, and what they learned did not match the details of the great war-god at all. It was almost the last straw when spectrographic analysis was applied to the warrior's black pigment and they found that, far from having been created by the ancient oxygenation and reducing process, they contained manganese, a chemical which was unknown to the Etruscans.

Finally, an old man was located in Rome who claimed that he had a hand in the making of the Metropolitan's three figures, and was able to prove it by producing a missing portion of one of them. In 1961, 40 years after the purchase, the 'Etruscan' Mars vanished from the public rooms of the museum to take its place among the ranks of the world's great forgeries.

Nowadays it is harder than ever for a forger to impose on anyone with the resources to investigate his work fully. Scientific techniques have been developed which can isolate modern elements in an alloy or pigment, thermo-luminescence will indicate whether clay was fired recently or long ago, carbon-14 will give the age of organic materials with a small margin of error, and high-powered microscopes will show up the tell-tale marks of contemporary tools and processes.

Every year of research produces more obstacles to the successful practice of the counterfeiter's craft, but if the difficulties are increasing the rewards are greater than they have ever been as prices continue to escalate. There are still enough buyers who are dishonest enough to enjoy the idea of stealing a march on hidebound officialdom and credulous enough to believe that the antiquities they are surreptitiously offered are the real thing. Every ancient civilisation has been the subject of inept copies by petty crooks and their victims have only themselves to blame when they are cheated into purchasing a worthless modern pastiche. These small-time forgers are in a very different class from the craftsmen who succeeded for years in deceiving the world's greatest authorities and who – such is human nature – compel a certain sneaking admiration for their nefarious deeds because they so nearly got away with it.

The Castellani sarcophagus, the work of the Pinellis, was bought by the British Museum and enjoyed pride of place in the Etruscan collection until it was exposed as a fraud in the 1930s. The organisation of illegal excavators supplies a channel for distributing and marketing such objects without the excavation 'pedigree' which helps to safeguard against frauds.

Bibliography

Introduction: the science of archaeology
Ceram, C. W. *Gods, Graves and Scholars* London 1952
Childe, V. G. *What Happened in History* Harmondsworth, 1942
Daniel, Glyn *The Origins and Growth of Archaeology* Harmondsworth, 1967
Hawkes, Jacquetta *The World of the Past* London, 1963
Finegan, Jack *Light from the Ancient Past* Princeton, 1946
Wheeler, Mortimer *Archaeology from the Earth* Oxford, 1954
Wilson, D. *Atoms of Time Past* London, 1975
Gilbert, Charles-Picard *Larousse Encyclopedia of Archaeology* Feltham, 1972

Theseus and the Minotaur: new light on the legend
Cottrell, Leonard *The Bull of Minos* London, 1953
Graham, James Walter *The Palaces of Crete* Princeton, 1962
Hawkes, Jacquetta *The Dawn of the Gods* London, 1968
Higgins, Reynold *The Archaeology of Minoan Crete* London, 1973
Hutchinson, R. W. *Prehistoric Crete* Harmondsworth, 1962

Pompeii and Herculaneum
d'Arms, J. H. *Romans on the Bay of Naples* Harvard, 1970
Deiss, J. J. *Herculaneum* London, 1966
Franciscis, A. de *Pompeii-Herculaneum. Guide with Reconstructions* Rome, 1964
Grant, Michael *Cities of Vesuvius* London, 1971
Leppmann, W. *Pompeii in Fact and Fiction* London, 1968
McKay, A. G. *Greek and Roman Domestic Architecture* London, 1972
Maiuri, A. *Pompeii, Ercolano e Stabia* Novara, 1961
Wheeler, R. E. M. *Roman Art and Architecture* London, 1964

The Rosetta Stone deciphered
Aldred, Cyril *Ancient Peoples and Places: The Egyptians* London, 1961
Ceram, C. W. *Gods, Graves and Scholars* London, 1952; *A Picture History of Archaeology* London, 1958
Gardiner, A. *Egypt of the Pharaohs* Oxford, 1961

The jungle cities of the Maya
Burland, Cottie *The People of the Ancient Americas* Feltham, 1970
Bushnell, G. H. S. *Ancient Arts of the Americas* London, 1965
Hagen, Victor W. von *In Search of the Maya* London, 1973

Kubler, G. *Art and Architecture of Ancient Americas* Harmondsworth, 1963
Morley, Sylvanus G. *The Ancient Maya* Stanford, 1956
Stephens, J. L. *Incidents of Travel in Central America* New York, 1841; *Incidents of Travel in Yucatán* New York, 1843
Thompson, J. E. S. *The Rise and Fall of Maya Civilisation* London, 1956

Chichén Itza: treasures from the sacred well
Boland, C. M. *They all Discovered America* New York, 1961
Camp, L. S. & C. C. de *Ancient Ruins and Archaeology* New York, 1965
Coe, M. D. *The Maya* London, 1966
Kubler, G. *Chichén Itzá and Tula* Harmondsworth, 1963
Reed, A. M. *The Ancient Past of Mexico* New York, 1966
Thompson, E. H. *People of the Serpent* New York, 1932
Willard, T. A. *City of the Sacred Well* New York, 1926

The epic of Gilgamesh
Frankfort, H. *The Birth of Civilisation in the Near East* London, 1951
Kramer, S. N. *History begins at Sumer* New York, 1957
Oppenheimer, A. L. *Ancient Mesopotamia* Chicago, 1964
Pritchard, J. B. *The Ancient Near East* Princeton, 1855; *Ancient Near Eastern Texts relating to the Old Testament* Princeton, 1955
Smith, G. *Assyrian Discoveries* London, 1875
Woolley, Leonard *Ur of the Chaldees* London, 1921; *Excavations at Ur* London, 1955

The mysterious civilisation of the Indus Valley
Basham, A. L. *The Wonder that was India* London, 1954
Marshall, John *Mohenjo-daro and the Indus Civilisation* London, 1931
Piggott, Stuart *Prehistoric India* London, 1950
Roy, S. *The Story of Indian Archaeology 1784–1947* Delhi, 1961
Wheeler, Mortimer *Still Digging* London, 1956; *Ancient Peoples and Places: Early India and Pakistan* London, 1959; *Civilisations of the Indus Valley and Beyond* London, 1966; *A Hundred Years of Indian Archaeology* (contributions by a cultural forum) Delhi, 1961

Jericho: the first city dwellers
Albright, W. F. *The Archaeology of Palestine* London, 1949
Anati, E. *Palestine before the Hebrews* New York, 1963

Braidwood, R. J. *The Near East and the Foundations for Civilisation* Oregon, 1952
Frankfort, H. *The Birth of Civilisation in the Near East* London, 1951
Kenyon, Kathleen M. *Digging up Jericho* London, 1957

Tutankhamun: the boy king
Aldred, Cyril *Jewels of the Pharaohs* London, 1971; *Akhenaten, Pharaoh of Egypt* London, 1968
Bratton, F. G. *A History of Egyptian Archaeology* London, 1967
British Museum *Treasures of Tutankhamun* (exhibition catalogue) London, 1972
Carter, H. *The Tomb of Tut-Ankh-Amen* (3 volumes, vol. 1 with A. C. Mace) London, 1923–33
Desroches-Noblecourt, C. *Tutankhamen: Life and Death of a Pharaoh* London, 1963
Engelbach, R. (Ed.) *Introduction to Egyptian Archaeology* Cairo, 1947
Fox, P. *Tutankhamun's Treasure* London, 1951
Montet, Pierre *Eternal Egypt* New York, 1964

The Dead Sea Scrolls
Aharoni, Y. *The Land of the Bible* London, 1967
Allegro, John M. *The Dead Sea Scrolls* Harmondsworth, 1956
Bright, J. *A History of Israel* London, 1972
Cross, F. *The Ancient Library of Qumran and Modern Biblical Studies* London, 1961
Driver, G. R. *The Judaean Scrolls* Oxford, 1965
Milik, J. T. *Ten Years of Discoveries in the Wilderness of Judaea* London, 1959
Vaux, Roland de *Archaeology and the Dead Sea Scrolls* London, 1973

Fakes, Frauds and Forgeries
Arnau, F. *Three Thousand Years of Deception in Art and Antiques* London, 1961
Jeppson, L. *Fabulous Frauds* London, 1971
Kurz, O. *Fakes* New York, 1967 (2nd Ed.)
Reisner, G. *Fakes and Forgeries in the Fine Arts* New York, 1950
Savage, G. *Forgeries, Fakes and Reproductions* New York and Washington, 1963
Wraight, R. *The Art Game* New York, 1965

Acknowledgments

Photographs were provided by the following:
Ägyptisches Museum, Berlin 125 top; Aerofilms, Boreham Wood 17 top; Alinari, Florence 148; P. Almasy, Neuilly-sur-Seine 17 bottom, 53 top, 62 top, 63, 66, 67, 104; Archaeological Survey of India, New Delhi 105 bottom, 106, 107 bottom; Atkinson 16 top; J. Bottin, Paris 61, 73 top; British Museum, London 12–13 top, 26 top, 91, 94; British Museum Research Laboratory, London 16 bottom, 153 top; J. E. Bulloz, Paris 95; J. Allan Cash, London 23 bottom, 100, 116, 117 bottom, 141; J. E. Dayton, Guernsey 143; J. Dubout–Larousse 13 bottom; Dumbarton Oaks, Harvard University, Washington, D.C. 65; Mary Evans Picture Library, London 32, 33 bottom, 36 top, 55 bottom, 86–87, 87 top, 89 top; W. Forman Archive, London 42 bottom, 70–71; Photographie Giraudon, Paris 15 bottom; Griffith Institute, Ashmolean Museum, Oxford 122, 124, 126, 128, 132, 133, 137; Hamlyn Group Picture Library 8–9, 11 bottom, 30, 35, 42 top, 44, 56, 59, 92 centre, 127; Hamlyn Group–G. Portlock 58; Hirmer Verlag, Munich 10, 11 top, 20 bottom, 23 top, 25 top, 25 bottom, 29, 46, 49, 88, 89, 129, 130 top, 130 bottom, 131, 135, 152; Jericho Excavation Fund 108, 117 top, 118, 119 top, 119 bottom, 120, 121; I. Groth Kimball, Mexico City 62 bottom, 68–69, 78 bottom; Mansell Collection, London 15 top, 24 top, 38, 39 top, 48, 52, 84, 90 top, 90 bottom, 92 bottom, 113, 157; Mansell–Alinari 40–41, 140; Mansell–Anderson 36 bottom, 37, 45, 150–151, 156; Mansell–Brogi 39 bottom; Bildarchiv Foto Marburg 22; Metropolitan Museum of Art, New York 153 bottom, 154; Middle East Archive, London 110, 111, 144 bottom; Musée du Louvre, Paris 153; Museum of Central Asiatic Antiquities, New Delhi 96; Museum für Völkerkunde, Berlin 64; Palestine Exploration Fund 114, 115 top, 115 bottom; Peabody Museum, Harvard University, Cambridge, Massachusetts 78 top, 83 top; Peabody Museum, Harvard University–Hillel Burger 79 top, 80 top, 80 bottom, 81, 82 top, 82 bottom, 83 bottom; Peabody Museum, Harvard University–F. Orchard 79 bottom; Popperfoto, London 99, 144 top; J. Powell, Rome 26–27 bottom, 101 top, 101 bottom, 105 top, 107 top; Radio Times Hulton Picture Library, London 14, 18, 20 top, 33 top, 50, 54, 55 top, 86 top, 98, 145 bottom; Rapho–Serge de Sazo 12 bottom; Rapho–Sabine Weiss 138, 145 top, 146; Samivel 24 bottom; R. Sheridan, London 34, 147; H. Stierlin, Geneva 60 top, 60 bottom; Towneley Hall Art Gallery and Museum, Burnley 6; Vautier–Decool, Paris 74, 75; Roger–Viollet, Paris 21, 27 top, 28, 51, 53 bottom, 72–73, 125 bottom; ZEFA (UK), London 42–43, 102–103.

Index

*Numbers in italic type
refer to illustrations*

Académie Royale 50
Academy of Fine Arts and
 Sciences of Naples 37
Academy of Herculaneum
 37
Adh-Dhib, Muhammad
 142
Ages of archaeology,
 classification of 11–12
Ain Feshkha 140, 145
Akhenaten 129, *125*
Albright, Professor 144
Alcubierre, Rocco 33, 37
Alexander the Great 50,
 139
Alexandria 47, 48, 50
Allegro, John 146
Amenhotep II 124
American School of
 Oriental Research 112,
 142
Amnisos 22
Antiochus IV Epiphanes
 139
Antiquities Service,
 Jerusalem 144, 145
Aphaia, Temple of *152*
Arab Legion 144
Archaeological Survey of
 India 99
archaeomagnetism 15
Archanes 22
Assurbanipal 86, 92
Aten 129, *125*
Australian Institute of
 Archaeology 112

Babylon 91, *90*
Banerjee, N. 97
Biaggio, Father 36–7
Birch, Dr S. 85, 87
Bolonchen 69
Bonaparte, Caroline 37–8
Bonaparte, Joseph 37
Bourbourg, Charles
 Etienne Brasseur de 77
British Academy 112
British School of Archae-
 ology, Jerusalem 112
Bronze Age *see* Ages of
 archaeology
bull, representations in
 Minoan art 26–7, *18,
 26–7*
bull-leaping, Minoan
 27–8, *26–7*

Canopus, decree of 55
Canova, Antonio 149–50
Capitoline wolf 149,
 150–1
carbon-14 *see* radio-carbon
 dating
Carlos III, King 33
Carnarvon, Lord 128, 136
Carrera, Rafael 63
Carter, Howard 77, 126,
 128, 129, 133, 134, 136,
 128
Castellani Sarcophagus
 155, *157*

Catherwood, Frederick
 58, 59–61, 63–4,
 65–73, *56, 59*
Cellini, Benvenuto 149,
 8–9, 150–1
Chac Mool 73, *68*
Champollion, Jean-
 François 50–5, *52*
Chardin, Jean *12*
Cheops 125, 126
Chicago Exhibition of
 1893 78
Chichén Itzá 69–73, 78,
 79–83, *67, 70–1, 72,
 73, 75, 78, 79, 80, 81,
 82, 83*
Cleopatra 50, 51
Cogolludo, Diego Lopez
 de 57, 69
Collège de France 52
Copán 59–60, 61, 63, 65,
 62, 74
Crete 19, 21–9, *18, 21,
 22, 23, 24, 25, 26–7, 28
 and see individual sites*
Cuidad Real, Fray
 Antonio de 57
Cunningham, Sir
 Alexander 97
Curzon, Lord 97

Dahshur, pyramid 126
Darwin, Charles 13
Davis, Theodore 128, 129,
 133
Dead Sea Scrolls 139, 141,
 142–7, *138, 144, 145,
 146, 147*
Deir el-Bahari 123, 124
Deluge, Chaldean account
 of 87, 93, 95 *and see*
 Gilgamesh
demotic script 48, 49, 50,
 55, *54*
dendrochronology 16–17
Denon, Vivant *48*
Dossena, Alcea 152–4
Douglass 17

Egypt, ancient 47, 50, 51,
 52, 55, 97, 109, 123–36,
 48, 49, 51, 53 and see
 Rosetta Stone *and*
 Tutankhamun
Elbeuf, Prince d' 32
Elgin, Lord 149
Eneberg 94
Evans, Sir Arthur 21, 22,
 24, 26, 27, 28, *18*

Fasoli 153, 154
Fiorelli, Guiseppe 31, 38,
 39, 40, 45
Fourier, J.-B. 50
Furtwängler, Professor
 152

Garstang, Professor John
 114, *114*
Gilgamesh 87, 93, 95, *92,
 94, 95*
Gizeh, Great Pyramid
 125–6
Gladstone, William 87

Graham, Professor J. 29

Haghia Triada 22, *24*
Harappa 98, 99, 105, *104*
Henry, Colonel 91
Herculaneum 11, 31,
 32–3, 36, 37, 44–5, *30,
 33, 42–3*
Hetep-heres 126, 134
hieroglyphic script 47, 48,
 49, 50, 51, 52, 55, *49, 54*
Hippodamus of Miletus 38
Hochman 151, 152
Horapollon 51

Indus Valley civilisation
 97–107, *96, 99, 100,
 101, 104, 105, 107 and
 see* Harappa *and*
 Mohenjo-daro
Iron Age *see* Ages of
 archaeology
Izdubar *see* Gilgamesh

Jericho 109–21, *108, 110,
 111, 113, 114, 115, 116,
 117, 118, 119, 120, 121*
Judaea 139 *and see* Dead
 Sea Scrolls

Kando 142, 144, 145
Karnak 47, *46, 49*
Kenyon, Dame Kathleen
 109, 112, 114, 120
Kircher, Athanasius 47
Knossos 21–9, *22, 23, 24,
 25, 26–7*
Kukulcan 72

Landa, Fray Diego de 77,
 78
Laocoön *10*
Layard, Sir Henry 92, *89*
Lendle, Professor O. 29
Lepsius, Richard 55
Libby, W. F. 14, 15
Linear B tablets 22
Luxor 47

Maccabees 139
Mahdia, Roman treasure
 ship 7, *11*
Maiuri, Professor 44
Mallia 21, 29
Marshall, Sir John 97–8
Masada 141
Maya civilisation 57–73,
 77–83, *56, 58, 59, 60,
 61, 62, 63, 64, 65, 66,
 68, 72, 73, 75, 76, 78,
 79, 80, 81, 82, 83 and
 see individual sites*
Meidum, pyramid 126
Menou, General 48
Merytamun, Queen 124–5
Mesopotamia 85, 87,
 88–93, 95, 98, 109
Minoan civilisation *see*
 Crete
Minos, king 19; stone
 chair of 24
Mohenjo-daro 97–8,
 99–105, 106–7, *17, 96,
 100, 101, 102–3, 105, 107*

Montezuma 82
Mosul 88, 93, 94, *86–7*
Murat, Joachim 37
Mycenae 19–21, *20*

Napoleon Bonaparte 38,
 47, 50, 51, 97, *48, 51*
Nerou Chani 22
Nineveh 87, 88, 91, 93,
 94, 121, *88, 89, 91*

Old Testament, Qumran
 manuscript 141, 147
 and see Dead Sea
 Scrolls
Olduvai Gorge, remains
 from 15
Oxford University
 Committee for
 Advanced Studies 112

Palenque 57, 63, 64–5,
 60, *61*
Palestine Exploration
 Fund 112, 114
Passionai, Cardinal 37
Petra, de 40
Phaistos 22, *21*
Pinelli family 155, *156,
 157*
Pliny the younger 31
Pompeii 11, 31, 32, 36, 37,
 38–40, 41–4, 45, *34,
 35, 36, 37, 38, 39,
 40–1, 42, 44, 45*
potassium-argon dating
 15
Psusennes I 124
Ptolemy V Epiphanes 50,
 51

Qumran 139–41, *146,
 147, 141, 144 and see*
 Dead Sea Scrolls

radio-carbon dating 14–
 15, 17, 106, *16*
Rameses VI 128, 133
Rashid *see* Rosetta 47
Rawlinson, Sir Henry 85,
 86, 87, 94, *86*
Reisner, G. A. 125
Riccardi family 155–6
Richter, Professor Gisela
 155
Rockefeller, John D. 145,
 147
Rosetta 47, *55*
Rosetta Stone 47–9,
 51–2, 55, 85, *54, 55*
Rothschild, Baron de 152
Royal Anthropological
 Institute 112
Royal Engineers, excava-
 tions at Jericho 114
Ruchomovsky, Israel 150,
 151, 152, 154, *153*
Ruggiero 40
Russel Trust, the 112

Saad, Joseph 144
Saitaphernes tiara 150–2,
 153
Santorini 22

Schliemann, Heinrich
 19–20, 21, 142, *20*
Schumann 156
Seleucus Nicator 139
Shani, D. 97
Sharpe, Samuel 86
Smith, George 85–95, *87*
Sneferu 126
Society of Antiquaries 49
Society of Biblical
 Archaeology 86, 87
Sogliano 40
Stabliae 31
Stephens, John Lloyd 57,
 58–61, 63–4, 65–73, 77
Stern, Professor von 152
Stone Age *see* Ages of
 archaeology

Tacitus 31
Taxila 98
thermoluminescence
 15–16
Theseus and the
 Minotaur, legend of 19,
 24, 29
Thompson, Edward
 Herbert 77, 78–83, *78*
Thorwaldsen, Albert
 Bertel 149, *152*
Thucydides 7
Thutmose III 124
Tiy, Queen 136
Tollund Man 139
tomb-robbers, ancient
 Egyptian 123–4, 125,
 126, 128, 134
'Toreador Fresco',
 Knossos 26
tree-ring dating *see*
 dendrochronology
Trever, Dr J. C. 142
Troy 19
Tutankhamun 77, 123,
 126–36, *122, 125, 126,
 127, 128, 129, 130, 131,
 132, 133, 135, 137*
Tylissos 22

Ur 95, 98
Uxmal 57, 69, *62, 63, 66*

Valley of the Kings 123,
 126, 128, 129, 133, 136,
 124
Vespasian, Emperor 141

Waldeck, Count Fréderic
 de 57–8, *58*
Weber, Charles 37
Wheeler, Sir Mortimer
 99, 100, 101, 106, *99*
Winckelmann, Johann 11,
 37, *33*
Woolley, Sir Leonard 95,
 99, *98*

Young, Thomas 49–50,
 50
Yum Chac 78, 79, 80

Zakro 22
Zoffany, Johann *6*